The Complete Book of Snooker

Others books by Eddie Charlton
Winning Snooker
Eddie Charlton's Trick Shots

The Complete Book of

Snooker

EDDIE CHARLTON

incorporating Winning Snooker and Trick Shots

DAVID & CHARLES

Newton Abbot   London

British Library Cataloguing in Publication Data
Charlton, Eddie
    The Complete Book of Snooker: incorporating
    Winning snooker and Trick shots.
    1. Snooker
    I. Title II. Charlton, Eddie.
    Winning snooker III. Charlton Eddie. Trick shots.

    794.7-35   GV900.S6
    ISBN 0-7153-8735-9

First published in Great Britain by David & Charles 1987

Printed in Hong Kong
for David & Charles Publishers plc
Brunel House   Newton Abbot   Devon

Foreword

Les Wheeler
Sporting Editor, *The Sydney Morning Herald*

The Complete Book of Snooker, by Eddie Charlton, is a classic of instruction; simply, honestly and skilfully presented by a master of the game.

Eddie is eminently qualified because he ranks with the fabulous Lindrums among champion Australian cuemen. He has dominated Australian snooker since the early 1960s and holds the world open championship and the World Matchplay Championship. In the fiercely competitive international scene he has been runner-up in the world professional championship twice and has won the popular BBC television series *Pot Black* three times.

Eddie's brilliant career record includes the remarkable feat of having beaten eight world champions — Horace Lindrum, Fred Davis, John Pulman, John Spencer, Alex Higgins, Ray Reardon, Terry Griffiths and Steve Davis.

Eddie was only nine when the magic of snooker captured him; that same magic which has enchanted you and me and millions of others.

He had the use of a family table at his hometown, Swansea, the coastal resort between Sydney and Newcastle in NSW. More importantly, at that tender age, he enjoyed the tuition and encouragement of a beloved grandfather.

Eddie was 15 when I first met him and the trademarks of his playing style: the keen eye, concentration and determined jut of the jaw were already evident. The foundation to success had been laid, and that Eddie capitalised on it is now just as evident.

Hard work were the key words to that success. Hard work in the coalmines to earn a living, hard work to develop natural sporting skills at surfing, football and boxing; hard work to absorb the intricacies of snooker technique and, hardest work of all, to cultivate the cue action and co-ordination so necessary to take him to the top of his ultimate profession.

Such was the background to the events, the man and the knowledge he acquired which resulted in *The Complete Book of Snooker*, by Eddie Charlton.

The lessons that you are about to study are those which the author accorded his sons, Edward and Michael. Both are century break players.

That, I believe, qualifies my opening statement about the honesty of this work. The simplicity and skill will be obvious in the following pages of excellent colour photography and absorbing instruction.

The Complete Book of Snooker will certainly increase your understanding of this wonderful game and, with dedication, your performance at the table.

I sincerely hope that you derive as much delight and benefit from Eddie Charlton's book as I was delighted and proud to contribute this foreword.

1983

Contents

My Life with Snooker

I started playing the game of snooker in my grandfather's billiards room as a nine-year-old schoolboy. My grandfather introduced me to the game because he was a very keen billiards and snooker man and had been in and around billiards rooms almost all his life. He was a wonderful little man, the best friend I ever had, and I loved him immensely. It was not difficult for him to get me started on snooker, and to keep me at it. I used to practise long hours and I thought so much of my grandparents that I lived with them for almost seven years. I practised before going to school, during lunch hour, and played for hours and hours in the afternoons and evenings.

My grandfather organized a game for me with the late and great Walter Lindrum, when Walter was playing for the war effort and the Red Cross at Anthony Hordern's big store in Pitt Street, Sydney in 1940. I was 11 years old. Playing before a crowd of 800-odd people was a great experience. It captured my imagination and I have been caught up by it all ever since.

I played most other sports during my school days into my youth and as a younger man. I played 27 years of football, and had a similar number of years surfing. I trained very hard all the year round. I played cricket, tennis, golf, and was in amateur boxing for about eight years. I had the great experience of boxing four rounds with Dave Sands who, at that time, was the British Commonwealth Middleweight Boxing Champion, as well as the Australian Middleweight, Light-heavyweight and Heavyweight Champion.

I was in an athletic club and that led to my being one of the carriers of the Olympic Torch from Darwin to Melbourne for the Olympic Games. I had a long sporting career and was always busy with various games, but I never did get away from the game of snooker. I travelled to Sydney to play competition games and exhibitions. I joined the Amateur Billiards Association and was fortunate enough to win three amateur snooker titles and one amateur billiards title.

I turned professional in 1960, became very keen on the game around about 1965 and, in 1968, after 22 years of working as an engineering fitter in and around coal mines, I became a full-time snooker professional.

My biggest thrill in the game was winning the Australian Professional Snooker Championship for the first time. I think it was an even bigger thrill than winning the Australian Senior Surfboat Championship, which we won at Coolangatta in 1950.

Winning the World Open Snooker Title against Rex Williams of England at the St George Leagues Club in Sydney in 1968 was another great experience, as was defeating Ray Reardon in the final of the World Matchplay Snooker Championship, in Melbourne in December 1976.

My outstanding achievement, I think, in the game was to make a 272 break at snooker. I think it is a record that will stand forever in the game of snooker because of the various things that would have to happen to beat my break. The 272 at snooker came, when I was on tour playing for the Royal N.S.W. Institute for Deaf and Blind Children, at the Kempsey Crescent Head Country Club, N.S.W. I had to play two opponents a game of snooker each. I broke the balls in the first frame, made a red into the centre pocket, and cleared the table for a break of 137. My new opponent came to the table, the referee re-racked the balls and I potted a red into the same pocket and cleared the table again a second time for a break of 135, making a world record running break of 272. Neither opponent had a shot.

I don't think I will ever do anything more outstanding than that in the game of snooker, and I don't think anybody else will either. Most of the old time greats that have heard about it have told me that they think it is the most outstanding event that has ever happened on a billiard table. To beat my record, a player would have to be playing different opponents, as I was, to be able to make the two opening breaks. Goodness knows what the odds are against making a red off the break twice, and then clearing two complete frames of snooker balls without allowing your opponent a single shot. My break of 272 is only 22 points below the possible for two complete frames of snooker. I would certainly like to be present to see the break that beats it.

I had another wonderful experience when I was playing Ray Reardon over a long tour of New Zealand (something like 273 frames of snooker). In one afternoon's play in Christchurch, I broke the balls in the very last frame of the session (we had an afternoon and night session to play), and Ray cleared the table, making a break of 139. Frank Holz, the organizer and compere of our tour and a former President of the N.Z. Amateur Billiards Association, checked up during the break between the end of that afternoon session and the evening session and found that Ray had established a record snooker break for competitive play in New Zealand of 139.

That night before commencing the evening's play, Frank announced: 'In the last frame this afternoon, Ray Reardon set a New Zealand record of 139 at snooker for competitive play. Now we are going to see Eddie Charlton beat that break with a break of 140!' Everybody laughed about that, including myself. Well, you would not want to know. Ray broke the balls and I commenced my break. I finished up clearing the table and my break finished exactly on 140 which then re-created a new New Zealand snooker record break for competitive play. Ray spent the rest of the tour telling everybody how he held the New Zealand record for about 2 hours. It was a hard break that I made, and during the building of the break I had to count to see the colours that I would take in order to finish in front of Ray's break of 139. It meant that, when some of my shots did not go the way I wanted, I had to pick the right balls (not necessarily the easiest balls) to at least finish with a break of 140. I managed to do it, and that again was a great thrill for me.

Playing against Warren Simpson in the Australian Matchplay Snooker Championship at Shoalhaven Ex-Servicemen's Club at Nowra in N.S.W., I made a break of 141 which is an all-time Australian record for championship play. That record stands as the N.S.W. record as well, so along with those two, I hold the record breaks in snooker for competitive play in Queensland, Western Australia and Victoria.

I had the great experience of making 110 break on *Pot Black* and that is the highest snooker break ever made in competitive play on television. To that date (December 1972) and that 110 break still stands as the highest break to date on '*Pot Black*'. I have no doubt that one day it will be beaten. I like playing television competitions, and television has done so much for our game. When television tournaments come along, I am always very keen to play in them.

Well, from all this background, here is my book, *The Complete Book of Snooker*. I have not asked any player to do anything that I do not do myself. I have copied the styles of various other players over the years. I have employed the good points that I have seen, in my game, and have dismissed the bad points. I have tried them all, and I only ask people to play snooker the way I play it. I think it is the easiest way to play the game, and if you are keen and dedicated enough to practise the shots shown in my book, time and time again until you perfect them, then you should make a good snooker player.

Merely applying some of the principles I outline may improve your game quickly, but snooker is the most demanding, exacting and difficult ball game played, and if you want to be an outstanding snooker player, then you have got to recognize this before you even start. Be prepared to practise the long hours needed and dedicate yourself to the task of becoming a good snooker player.

Snooker is a wonderful game. It has taken me around the world several times. I have been to the United Kingdom on many occasions in fact and have played over the whole of that country, in Canada twice and the United States three times. I have played extensive tours through New Zealand, Papua New Guinea, Sri Lanka, India, and I have also played in Malta, Singapore, Hong Kong, Rome, Milan, Genoa and Amsterdam, as well as touring South Africa.

I have met some wonderful people in my travels and I have always thoroughly enjoyed the game. I still enjoy the game should I lose a match. The things that I always try to do are play the game well, and leave a good impression wherever I go.

EDDIE CHARLTON
1983

Eddie Charlton with his sons Edward (left) and Michael.

Eddie Charlton's Record

CURRENT TITLES HELD:

World Matchplay Snooker Champion

World Open Snooker Champion

British Commonwealth Open Snooker Champion

Australasian Professional Snooker Champion

Australian Matchplay Snooker Champion

Australian Professional Snooker Champion

Australian Professional 14.1 Pocket Billiards Champion (American Straight Pool)

N.S.W. Professional Snooker Champion

N.S.W. Open Snooker Champion

World Champion of Champions (Billiards, Snooker, Pool)

Winner of International television *Pot Black* series — 1972, 1973 and 1980

Winner of Australian television *Super Snooker* series — 1974

Winner of Yorkshire television *Celebrity Snooker* — 1976

Winner of 20 television tournaments, by far the largest number of any other player.

HOLDER OF UNIQUE WORLD RECORD:

Two consecutive breaks at snooker of 137 and 135 without either opponent getting a shot, making a world record running break of 272.

NUMBER OF CENTURY OR OVER SNOOKER BREAKS MADE TO DATE: 2882

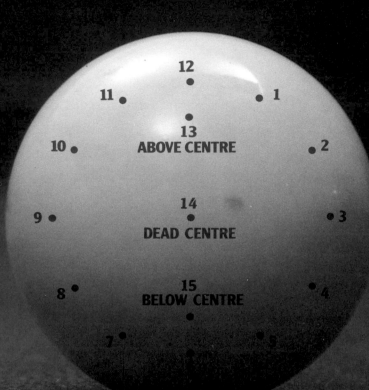

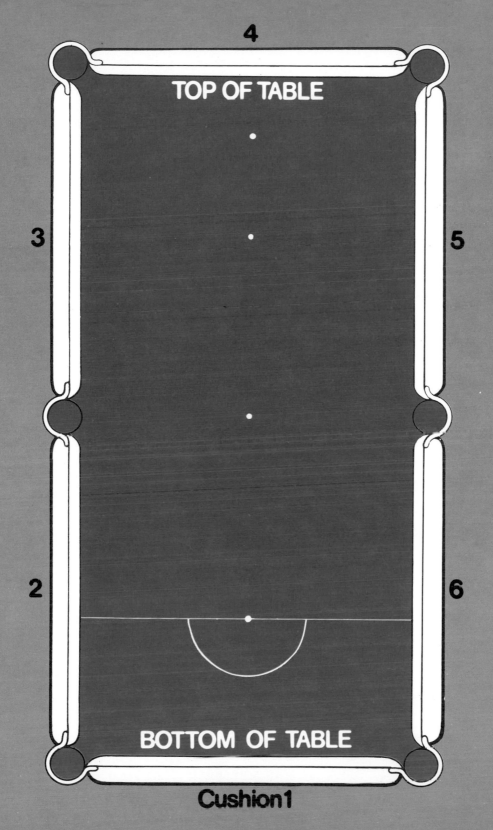

TOP OF TABLE

4

3

5

2

6

BOTTOM OF TABLE

Cushion1

9

Equipment

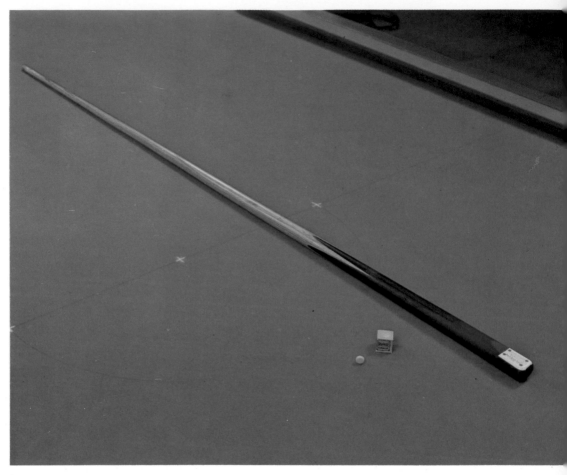

3

The Cue

No one can play good snooker if the material is not correct. The cue is of the utmost importance. It should reach (when placed perpendicular on the floor) to 2.5 cm (1") below the shoulder. That applies equally whether the player be 150 cm (5') or 180 cm (6') in height. The weight should not be less than 16 oz. Many players may prefer a lighter weight, but leading professionals shun anything lighter.

Try and secure your own private cue. The cue should be of a preferred weight, be well balanced and taper from butt end to tip end. I prefer a ⅜″ tip and ferrule size for the full size 2¹/₁₆″ snooker balls. Do not, under any circumstances, use a cue that is whippy. Select one that is nearly rigid. If the balance is right, the weight of the cue will be distributed evenly. Try to avoid a cue that is top heavy at the tip end. A well balanced cue has its balance point approximately where the butt points meet the shaft. The weight of the cue is important and should suit the feel of the individual player. For instance, if a player said to me: 'I think I prefer the weight of this 18 oz. cue against the 17 oz. that I just used', I would advise him to play with the 18 oz. cue.

My cue is 55″, weighs 17 oz. and has a ⅜″ tip and ferrule. It has a black ebony butt and an English ash shaft.

The Tip

To tip your cue, remove old glue from it and dress cue to a level surface by using a sharp, fine file. Use a firm to hard tip, avoiding one that is spongy. There are many good contact glues on the market today. Apply glue to cue and the back of the tip and affix when the glue begins to dry. Squeeze the tip on firmly and evenly. Turn cue upside down and press on an even surface to remove air bubbles, then leave to dry before trimming. When the tip is ready for trimming, use a small piece of sandpaper to remove the rough edges from around the surface (until it is like looking at the end of your forefinger) so that a rounded tip will be striking a round ball. I prefer Elk Master tips.

The Chalk

I hold my chalk before a heater to dry it and prevent it from greasing the cue ball. When a ball is heavily chalked, it kicks and throws unnatural angles. Use your chalk regularly and lightly as over-caking the tip with chalk prevents the tip from gripping the cue ball correctly, and the action of scrubbing the chalk onto the tip with force only wears away the tip. I prefer green Triangle chalk as it does not mark the cue ball. Both Elk Master tips and Triangle chalk are American products.

Snooker Terminology

LOSING HAZARD	Means to play the cue ball into a pocket after contact with an object ball (in snooker, a foul).
WINNING HAZARD	To pocket the object ball with the cue ball.
RUN THROUGH	To impart top spin on the cue ball by hitting it above centre so that its forward rotation will enable it to continue after contact on the object ball.
STUN THROUGH	To force the cue ball forward at speed in preference to a dead strength 'run through'.
STUN SHOT	To hold the cue with a very firm grip, stopping short in your cut delivery when striking the cue ball, i.e. to 'kill' any travel of the cue ball.
FORCING SHOT	To strike the cue ball with power.
DRAW SHOT	To draw the cue ball back towards the striker after contact with the object ball.
SCREW BACK	To cause the cue ball to spin backwards towards the striker after contacting with the object ball.
CUT SHOT	The fine cutting (feathering the edge) of the object ball.
TO POT	To pocket the object ball.
SWERVE SHOT	A shot brought into play when it is necessary to go around one or more balls to contact another.
MASSÉ	To be played for the same reason as a swerve shot. A quicker turn is desired when distances from the cue ball to the object ball are not sufficient for a swerve to be played.
CUE BALL	White ball — always to be struck with the cue tip.
OBJECT BALL	All other balls, i.e. reds and coloureds.
BRIDGE	Distance of cue from bridge hand thumb to cue tip.
SIDE	Means spin.
NAP	Means tiny fibres of wool each fitting into and overlapping the other, like scales on a fish. (West of England manufactured top quality cloth — Australian merino wool.)
DOUBLING	When an object ball strikes one or more cushions on its journey to a pocket.
PLANT SHOTS	Means one object ball, on to another object ball.
SNOOKERING	Means to cover the ball on by ball or balls not on.

Winning Snooker

PART

1

Contents (List of Lessons)

Correct Stance

Unless you are comfortable and theoretically right, you are actually starting from behind scratch. Every part of you, and the cue, must become one perfectly functioning unit.

Stance at the table is tremendously important. Unless you are comfortable and have placed the feet and body so that eye alignment is correct, all that follows will be false, and will cause many errors in your game.

Assuming you are a right-handed player and have placed your cue on the line that you consider will put the pot down, before chinning your cue for the correct stance, look straight down on your cue and make sure that your cue line is passing over your right instep. This ensures two very important things:

(a) that the cue arm is close to the body,
(b) that the head will be straight when chinning the cue.

The toe of the right shoe should be turned slightly right of square for comfort, and the right knee should never bend, as it is 'anchored' for steadiness and stability. The left shoe should point towards the line of the shot with the toe of the shoe turned slightly in for comfort. The knee of the left leg does bend, allowing your body balance to be forward over the bent left knee and your body weight should then be felt on your left foot. This is a very important point as most shots in snooker are 'follow throughs' and to cue accurately on 'follow through' shots, your body balance must be forward. The distance between the feet is only governed by height, as what you have to do is comfortably stretch out and chin your cue.

Two points to remember:

1. Assuming that your right foot is correctly under the line of the cue, and you feel a tendency to be off balance either way, then move the left foot either in or out depending on which way you may feel off balance. The right foot is not to be moved from under the cue line, unless you are left with an awkward lie such as leaning over the cushion or using the rest.
2. If, when chinning down your cue, you feel bunched up in the back or shoulders, then widen your feet until you are down chinning the cue, comfortably relaxed.

4 – Stance (Side)

Note: Cue tip – 13 mm (½″) from cue ball.

Cue – as near to horizontally level as possible.

Bridge Hand – firm grip of cloth carrying forward balance.

Bridge Arm – as straight as possible always.

Head – straight down chinning cue for good rifle-type sighting.

Cue Hand – grip cue butt where forehand drops straight from elbow.

Legs – comfortably apart – left knee bent, allowing weight to be shared with the bridge hand and right leg. Right leg straight, right instep below cue line.

5 – Stance (Feet)

The toe of the right shoe should be turned slightly forward of square for comfort and the right knee should never bend as it is 'anchored' for stance and stability. The left toe should bend towards the line of the shot with the toe of the shoe turned slightly in for comfort. The knee of the left leg does bend allowing your body to be forward over the bent left knee.

5   6

6 – Stance (Front)

Aiming at snooker is similar to aiming with a rifle, when the eye must run down the barrel for sighting at the target. So also in snooker must the eye run along the cue for sighting at the object ball. Plate 6 shows my head perfectly straight while chinning the cue. My bridge hand is firm and my bridge arm is straight. My cueing arm hangs straight from the elbow to the cue butt.

18

7 – Stance (Back)

7

In facing the shot and aligning the cue, the right foot, the cue, the cueing arm and the head are all on perfect line. The head is directly above the cue in line of aim. When the time comes to actually strike the cue ball, your eye should be fixed firmly on the object ball.

Aim

Sighting at snooker is similar to sighting with a rifle. A person, shooting with a rifle, when the time comes to squeeze the trigger, should be sighting at the target. The target in snooker is the object ball. Therefore, when the time comes to deliver the final stroke, the sighting should be on the object ball.

My sighting technique is:

1. To move into position behind the cue ball and position the feet while sighting over the cue ball at an area on the object ball that, when connected on by the cue ball, will send it on line to the pocket.
2. Place the bridge hand and align the cue tip firstly on the area on the cue ball that you intend to strike with the cue tip, and secondly seeing the cue ball on to the object ball that will send it off on line to the pocket.

Having comfortably set your stance, and got down to chinning your cue for good rifle sighting, you are now ready to commence cueing. When you commence cueing, the only moving parts in the whole of your body, other than your cueing arm, are your eyes. Move your eyes to the cue ball to make sure that your cue action is good and that you are in fact going to strike the cue ball where you intend to. When satisfied with that, raise your eyes (not your head) to the object ball, re-checking for a second time that your sighting on to the object ball is still correct. Continuing to cue in a short, flat, smooth, relaxed action, lower your eyes to the cue ball for the second time, re-checking for the second time that you are still going to strike the cue ball in the intended place with the cue tip. Raise your eyes for the third time to the object ball, re-checking for the third time your sighting on to that ball. Then, with your cue tip back to the cue ball, stop your cue for a brief pause, drop your eyes to the cue ball for the third and last time, making sure that your cue tip is still on to the intended area of the cue ball, before raising your eyes to the object ball for the fourth and last time. Concentrating your sighting onto the object ball at this stage, you should be actually staring at the area on the object ball that you intend to contact the cue ball on to, before pulling your cue back and delivering the stroke that sends the cue ball on its journey. This whole procedure has taken no more than 8 – 10 seconds, and your pause in cueing with your cue tip almost up to the cue ball has been quite brief, before delivering the final stroke.

Remember: When the time comes to stroke the cue ball, your eyes should be on the object ball. The three important things to have in mind while sighting –

(a) When sighting the object ball, you are saying to yourself, am I hitting this object ball in the right place?

(b) When sighting on the cue ball, am I hitting the cue ball on the area that I intend to with my cue tip?

(c) Finally, while your eyes have been concentrating from the cue ball to the object ball, you always have the feeling in mind regarding your cueing arm, as to how hard or how soft you are going to play the shot.

8 – Aim (Cue and Object Ball)

8

I have set up a shot that is just one of the many angles which occur in the game of snooker. Having set my stance and aligned my cue from the cue ball on to the object ball, I am now ready to commence cueing. You are seeing the shot lined up as I see it. I see the cue ball on a continuation of the line of my cue, against the object ball where the second cue ball is now.

9 –Aim (Object and Five Cue Balls)

The blue ball is to be pocketed into the centre pocket with any one of five cue balls set up at different angles. On attempting to pocket the blue ball on each of five occasions using a different cue ball for each shot, the point to be remembered is that every time you move behind a new cue ball, the potting angle is altering, but the contact point is the point on the object ball the blue ball, where you see the sixth cue ball.

9

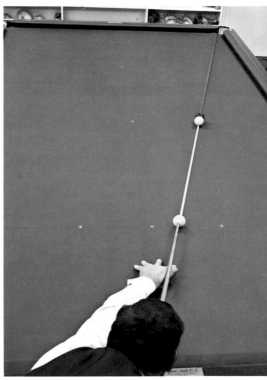

10

10 –Aim (Object and One Cue Ball)

This illustration shows the line of the cue to the cue ball, the white line of the cue ball to the object ball, and the red line of the object ball to the pocket. I have placed the second cue ball against the object ball, showing the contact point when the cue ball reached the object ball, sending the object ball on its journey to the pocket.

22

11 –Aim (Object and Two Cue Balls)

Plate 11 shows a second cue ball against the object ball illustrating my previously explained sighting technique of seeing the cue ball on a continuation of the line of my cue against the object ball when contact takes place.

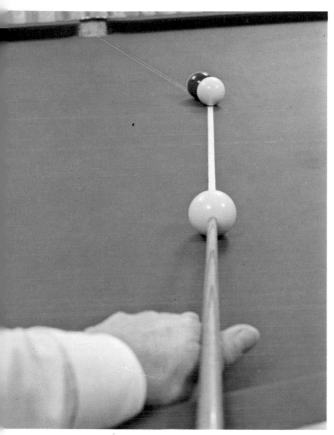

11

12

12 –Aim (Three Object and Four Cue Balls)

The picture shows three object and four cue balls, depicting the correct point from one cue ball to all three object balls, all at different angles to the pocket. The three cue balls placed against each of the three object balls show the desired contact point. You will see that the closest object ball is a straight pot (full ball contact). The second object ball is a half ball contact, and the third object ball is a fine cut (feathering the edge).

Cueing

Probably the most important point in the whole game of snooker is the correct striking of the cue tip onto the cue ball. There is no instance I can think of where a good cueist would not be a good player.

My aiming technique, if followed as I have laid down, is not at all difficult. With the practice and experience I have to this day, I can say that aiming at snooker does not cause me any concern at all. In fact I would say that if I had a machine to fire the cue ball for me, I would pot every ball I aimed at.

Cueing, however, will always be the art of the game. When I miss shots at snooker it is usually because of my cueing. That is where the human element comes in, and is the reason that, however hard a person may try, however long a person may practise, he cannot pot all the balls all the time.

Shots can be missed when it is not the player's fault! It can happen when a table is not level, allowing balls to run off. The nap on a cloth, running from baulk end to spot end, will turn slow moving balls from their true course, mainly across and against the nap. Again, balls running around on a dirty table can pick up chalk from cue tips which, having attached to a ball or balls, will cause a 'kick' on contact, resulting in the object ball breaking away from the cue ball at an incorrect angle.

These few points I mention are all part of the game, and have to be contended with. To play snooker consistently well, however, you certainly have to practise to develop a good cue action, and then work hard to maintain that action. In my lesson on aiming, you will recall my very important point of watching the object ball when the time comes to strike the cue ball. You may wonder how you can hit the cue ball in the correct place with the cue tip when you are not ever atching it.

The answer is, of course, good cueing. My technique is rely on my solid, comfortable stance, and my good cue action, to finally strike the cue ball at the intended point on its circumference, when I am not watching it. But if you recall I had checked on my cueing at the cue ball *three* times during my address, sighting, and while doing my preliminary cueing movements prior to striking the cue ball.

On moving into my shot, I concentrate on positioning my feet, placing my bridge hand, and aligning my cue – (a) to striking the cue ball where I intend to, and (b) to the area of the object ball that will send that object ball off on its journey towards the pocket.

Having comfortably taken my stance, aligned my cue and my aim, I am now ready to start cueing. With my cue tip approximately 13 mm (½″) from the cue ball at address, my length of backward stroke will be governed entirely by the power I intend putting into the shot.

Because my power does not come from the strength of the *grip* of my cue but, in

24

fact, from the drive of my cueing arm, it stands to reason that if I intend to play a soft stroke, the travel of my cue tip back from the cue ball will be *short*.

Because of the intended soft stroke, my bridge from bridge hand to cue ball would be shorter than normal. Having shortened up in front with my bridge hand, it follows that I will shorten up my gripping point on the butt of my cue with my cueing hand, by moving my grip forward. I play from on, or close to cushions the same way!

In your preliminary cueing movements, you should be aware of your cue finishing its forward stroke 13 mm (½″) back from the cue ball. Commence your back and forth cueing action in a steady, relaxed, unhurried manner. Keep your cue as horizontally level as possible. The only moving parts of the whole of your body should be your eyes (moving slowly and easily from cue ball to object ball, and back to cue ball as explained in my lesson on Aiming) and your cueing arm.

Your cueing arm is your forearm, wrist and fist, all swinging from your elbow as one unit. Do not develop a wristy action. There should be no wrist action at all, for any shot in snooker, if you follow my advice. There is to be no movement of your cue arm shoulder at all. Your cueing arm is to swing from the elbow only.

Your cue action should be a short, flat, back and forth motion, as relaxed, steady and as slow as you can manage, without losing the nice, smooth rhythm you should continually practise to develop into your technique.

There also is great timing required if you are to become a good cueist. Timing is absolutely essential, otherwise you will never consistently stroke your shots at the right speed. What follows then, of course, is that your intended distance of travel of the cue ball seldom works out as planned. The timing I speak of is between your eyes, and your cueing arm.

The occasions when I play well, which fortunately is most of the time, providing I am not mentally tired from late nights and excessive travelling, are the occasions that I am fresh and keen to play, and can have the three all important fundamentals of snooker working together in my mind and actions at the same time:
1.   While staring at the object ball and saying to myself: 'Yes, my aim is good, and I am going to hit the object ball in the right place to send it to the pocket'.
2.   While staring at the cue ball and saying to myself: 'Yes, my cue action is good, and I am going to strike the cue ball with the tip of my cue where I intend to'.
3.   While the concentration of my mind and eyes have been on the two balls concerned, I have always had the feel of my cue, in stroking back and forth during my preliminary movements, as to exactly how hard or how soft I am going to play the particular shot.

My sighting and cueing technique, from the time my stance was set and cue aligned, has taken 8–10 seconds.

Now, happy with all thoughts on this particular shot, when staring at the object ball for the third time, I stop my cue with the cue tip to within 13 mm (½″) of the cue ball, for the fraction of a second that it takes to lower my eyes to the cue ball. Then finally making sure that my cue tip is still going to strike the intended area on the cue ball, I raise my eyes back to the intended area on the object ball, and deliver my stroke by pulling back and finally playing forward, and through, the cue ball.

I have found that the slight pause has been invaluable in my play since the late and great Joe Davis (undefeated World Professional Snooker Champion for twenty years) offered me that advice whilst helping me with my game on my first visit to London in 1968.

Joe and I became very good friends over the years, and his advice to me on the 'pause' before striking is the best advice ever extended to me during my snooker-playing career.

The importance for me in the pause is that, after playing snooker for lengthy sessions over many frames during our big professional matches, I get mentally tired because of the concentration required. While all thoughts and concentration on this particular shot have been going through my mind and actions, the pause allows me to 'gather' in all those thoughts, steady myself, and actually rally strength before finally playing the stroke.

When cueing note:

(a)   The pause takes place with the cue tip up to within 13 mm (½″) of the cue ball
      — not at the back of the stroke!

(b)   Do not clutch the cue in a stranglehold with your cue hand. As firm a grip as it takes to wave your cue around in the air will suffice. Your power should not come from the grip of your cue, but from the feel, or drive, of your cue arm. If a soft shot is to be played, your cue action is a soft push. (Shorten your bridge, shorten your cue hold, shorten your stroke.)

(c)   If a power shot is to be played, your cue action is a smooth, controlled, rhythmic drive of the cue arm. (Lengthen your bridge — not more than 25 cm (10″) — move your hold position on the cue butt so that your forearm, wrist and fist, drop vertically from your elbow, when the cue tip is 13 mm (½″) from the cue ball.)

13 – Cueing (Grip, Taking Hold)

The grip being formed. When taking hold of the cue with the cue hand, you should wrap the fingers and thumb around the butt, thus pulling the butt up into the palm of the hand. Do not clutch or strangle the cue. The cue should lie in the middle pads of the four fingers. The grip is taken with the first two fingers and the thumb only. Your remaining two fingers close on to the butt without gripping.

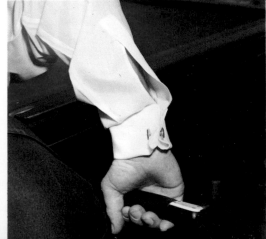

14 – Cueing (Grip, Inside View)

Plate 14 shows my cue hand gripping the butt of the cue with the first two fingers and the thumb. The remaining two fingers simply close on the butt. I maintain this grip for practically every shot that I play, as my power comes from the drive of my cueing arm and not from slackening or strengthening my grip.

15 – Cueing (Grip, Outside View)

The cue hand is shown taking the cue hold where the hand hangs straight from the elbow.

15

16 – Cueing (Grip, Back Stroke)

A normal stroke cue hand to cue ball 25 cm (10″) at the end of the backswing. My backswing on a normal stroke is 10 cm (4″). Note the cue is as near to level as possible.

16

17 – Cueing (Grip, Forward Stroke)

The cueing arm at the end of the forward stroke. Note my follow through of approximately 13 cm (5″). My follow through is short compared with most other professional players.

17

18 – Cueing (Grip, Back View)

The cue, right elbow, right hand and centre of the head are all on line to the cue ball. Cue hand hanging straight from the elbow allows for relaxed swinging of the cueing arm, and my thumb just brushes my hip while cueing.

18

19A – Cueing (Top Spin)

The bridge hand forms a cradle to carry the cue. The body weight is down on the palm of the hand, which grips the cloth with all four finger pads well spread for strength and stability. Forefinger points out to meet a well cocked thumb forming a cradle for the cue to run in. To address the cue tip to the top of the cue ball to apply top spin for follow through shots, note that the knuckles on the bridge hand are high and the cue just clears the cushion rails. Striking point on cue ball for follow through shots, 12 o'clock.

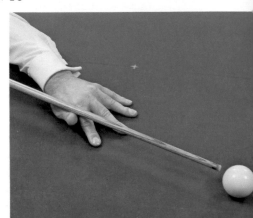

19A

19B – Cueing (Centre Striking)

To lower cue tip to the centre of the cue ball, do not lift your back cueing hand and the butt of the cue to get your tip down. To move from 12 o'clock cueing to dead centre striking on the cue ball, simply allow your bridge hand to flatten down, lowering your forefinger knuckle and thumb till cue tip is dead centre on the cue ball. Striking point on the cue ball, 14.

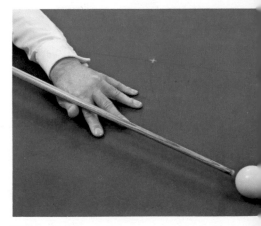

19B

28

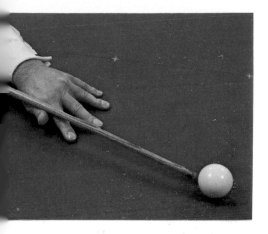

19C – Cueing (Stun Shots)

To lower cue tip, below dead centre, for most
stun shots again flatten bridge hand, and lower
knuckles until cue tip lowers to point 15 on the
cue ball.

19C

19D – Cueing (Deep Screw)

19D

Note bridge hand now. I have turned my wrist to get the weight of my forward
balance to the base of my bridge hand thumb, pads of first three fingers, and down
to the point of my little finger. The palm of bridge hand is now clear of the table.
Base of the thumb is on the cloth, and without raising the back cueing hand at all,
cue tip has been successfully lowered to the deep screw striking position on the cue
ball. Striking point for deep screw – 6 o'clock. When intending to apply severe back
spin for a deep screw shot, remember that you now intend striking down in the miscue area. Chalk your tip carefully before attempting this shot and be careful to send
your cue through, as previously advised, with a smooth, controlled, rhythmic drive
of the cue arm. When attempting this shot a firm grip of the cloth with your bridge
hand, and your cue with your cueing hand, is essential.

19E – Cueing
(Bridge Hand, Bridge Arm)

With your body weight forward over your bent left knee on to your bridge hand, you have to support your forward body weight by comfortably setting your bridge arm as straight from your shoulder, to your bridge hand, as is possible depending on the position of the cue ball or any other balls. Having set your stance with your right leg straight (braced against any movement backwards) and your straight left bridge arm (propping onto your bridge hand) those two anchor points will assist greatly in holding you steady against any backward or forward movement, particularly when applying power shots.

19E

20 – Cueing (Grip and Head)

Strength of grip for most shots I play is as firm as it takes to move the cue around

20

in the air. Slightly more strength than simply holding the weight of your cue, as now you are controlling your cue, and not your cue controlling you. I am only down in the cue ball addressing position a matter of seconds when the knuckles of my cueing hand turn white with the pressure that is being applied. All four finger pads are around the cue butt. My actual grip, with forearm hanging straight to the gripping position before commencing cueing, is actually being taken with the first two fingers and the thumb only. My back two fingers are simply closed on the cue butt. At the back of my back swing, my two back fingers are still on the butt of the cue, but have allowed the back of the palm of my hand to come off the cue, and the thumb and first two fingers are now in control of the cue. On coming back to strike the cue ball and follow through, my hand has closed allowing four fingers back on to the butt of the cue, but the actual grip is still being maintained by the thumb and first two fingers only.

Do not wrap your thumb around the cue. Allow your thumb to point straight down past the cue towards your right instep, and simply close your straight thumb onto the butt of the cue locking it there between the first two fingers. If you allow your thumb to grip around the cue at all, it will have a strong tendency to pull your cue off line when delivering your stroke.

When down on the stroke passing through the whole aiming and cueing technique, it is extremely important to keep your head absolutely straight and steady. By having my chin down to cue level I have rifle sighting aim and automatically, being a right eye sighter down the cue, my head is perfectly straight. While cueing, I continually feel the cue glancing back and forth under my chin tip. This is a guide for keeping my cue horizontally level, for keeping my head straight and my head, neck and shoulders, absolutely still.

If you feel you are getting head movement on the shot, it could be because you are getting shoulder movement or eye movement during your aiming and cueing activity. You can eliminate shoulder and upper arm movement quite simply by remembering three very important points:

(a) On sighting if you do not let your eyes move from the object ball, particularly on the final stroke, then your head cannot move.
(b) If you are concentrating on swinging your cueing arm from the elbow only, you cannot get upper arm or shoulder movement into the shot.
(c) Do not open and close your cueing hand on the cue butt. Your first two fingers and thumb are always gripping the cue. The back of your palm on your cueing hand, by easing off the cue butt on your backward motion, allows the cue to remain horizontally level during your cueing movements.

Bridging

When the cue ball is near the rail, always work on my principle of retaining, at all times where possible, the 10″ of bridge previously discussed. If your bridge hand can comfortably be placed down on the bed, between the cushion and cue ball, at the same time retaining 25 cm (10″) of bridge, then certainly adopt your bridge hand in that position.

It is always a distinct danger on any shot to play a stroke with too long a bridge. With the absolute importance of the accurate striking of the cue ball with the cue tip, it only stands to reason that anyone playing with a bridge of 35 cm – 41 cm (14″ – 16″), or even 51 cm (20″), between their bridge hand thumb and the cue ball, simply cannot be sure of where they are striking the cue ball. There is too much cue out from the sliding point on the bridge.

I see some players making shots with two feet of bridge to the cue ball. Do not fall into this category. Stay short, working as often as possible on my advice of a bridge distance of 25 cm (10″), shot, after shot, after shot!

Because of my very strong feeling regarding this point of correct snooker play, it is always the positioning of my bridge hand that determines the gripping point of my cue hand, onto the cue butt. Having set my bridge, as often as is possible, up to or within 25 cm (10″) of the cue ball, my cue hand grip will drop to the cue butt where my forearm drops straight from the elbow.

21 – Bridging (Out from Cushion)

If insufficient distance between cushion and cue ball prevents the placing of your bridge hand onto the bed of the table for a normal shot, causing an extremely short bridge (shown in later plates), it may suffice to withdraw your bridge hand so that the palm of your bridge hand is up on the edge of the cushion face, with your fingertips down on the bed. If I can adopt this position and only decrease my bridge length to say 23 cm (9″), I prefer to adopt this bridge hand position than one on top of the cushion rail, where the distance to the cue ball would be too great.

21

22 – Bridging (Close to Cushion)

The fingers are placed flat on the rail, and the cue slides between the first two fingers. The fingers close comfortably on the cue shaft to ensure accurate aiming. The thumb beneath the fingers running its length against the cue shaft serves as a guide. This is a good grip for locking the cue when playing a power shot from off cushions. Keep your cue as horizontally level as possible. Again, good cueing will be called for.

22

23 – Bridging (On Cushion)

When forced to play straight out from a cushion the cue ball is hard against, it is now impossible to maintain your 25 cm (10″) of bridge because your bridge hand would not even be on the cushion. I am now forced to move my bridge hand fingers to the very outside edge of the cushion rail. Because my little finger is shorter, I allow it to drop off the rail. By doing this my bridge hand will be back 2.5 cm (1″) further. Although I have now placed my three bridge hand fingers to the top outside edge of the cushion rail, I still have my stance set allowing forward balance over my bent left knee, through my straight bridge arm on to my bridge hand fingers. I am forced to shorten my bridge to approximately 13 cm (5″) and because of shortening my bridge, I shorten my cue hold on the butt of the cue.

Note that my cue hold has now gone forward along the cue butt and that my forearm from elbow to cue hand is forward of vertical. This is one of the few occasions that my cue arm will be forward of vertical. Because I have had to shorten my bridge, I must shorten my stroke. When playing from a position like this, I seldom try to use a forcing shot because I am already in an extremely difficult situation.

To afford myself every chance of playing a good shot, I chalk my cue carefully before adopting this stance. I now allow the butt of the cue to simply cradle in the pads of my four fingers, I relax my grip so that my fingers only are carrying the weight of the cue, and I play most shots with a soft, smooth *push*. I let the cue do the work; I seldom try to play a forcing stroke. I seldom worry overmuch about position for the next shot from this awkward situation because I am content to only pot the ball on this occasion, as my next shot is not going to be as difficult anyway.

A final word of advice on this situation. Try to be careful while cueing, and in delivering your final stroke, not to allow the tip or the bridge of your cue to make

contact with the cushion rail. Do not lift your back hand to raise the butt of your cue (thus allowing better striking of the cue tip down onto the cue ball) any more than you have to.

23

24

25

26A

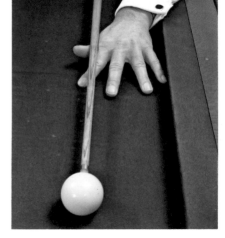

26B

34

26C

24 – Bridging (Across Left)

When forced to play from this position, do not lift the cue butt any higher than you have to. Be careful that your cue tip does not touch the cushion rail before making contact with the cue ball. Having chalked your tip carefully before addressing the shot, try to be content in playing a soft shot which will ensure a smooth delivery.

25 – Bridging (Across Right)

Playing off the cushion rail at this angle affords me a much easier opportunity of striking the cue ball correctly than the previous plate showed. Now, being a right-handed player, it is more comfortable to adopt my normal stance, locking my cue along the cushion rail as shown and to use the top of the cushion cloth in this instance as a guide for my cue shaft. I am very careful to have my bridge hand fingers locking the cue so that there will be no movement off the cue line of my cue while, in this instance, cueing across the cushion rail. When cueing along and near to the cushion rail, the next three plates will show my recommended bridge hand positions.

26A – Bridging (Along)

The cue ball even closer to the cushion on a similar shot. Now, with insufficient room to have the palm of bridge hand and all fingers down on to the table, I have allowed two of my fingers to remain in contact on the bed with my forefinger and thumb retaining the normal trough for my cue to run in. My last two fingers are placed up on and along the cushion rail for absolute comfort and stability.

26B – Bridging (Along)

I have sufficient room to place my bridge hand in the normal position, however you will note that I have had to bend my elbow to comfortably place my bridge hand in this position, when aligning the cue for the shot to be played.

26C – Bridging (Along)

The cue ball is now hard against the cushion with the shot to be played along the cushion rail. From this position I cannot retain two fingers on the table bed. Now I adopt the 'boucle' grip by placing my middle finger down on the bed cloth, my last two fingers on top of the cushion rail as before, while making a loop around the cue by my forefinger meeting my thumb. The cue runs against my middle finger and thumb and is held firmly and guided by the inside loop of my forefinger.

27A, B – Awkward Bridging (Off Cushions, Right and Wrong)

27A

27B

This is a difficult shot. Only the top of the cue ball is there to contact. To make sure of hitting what we can see of it, we have to be careful of our grip and cue action. Most players in this position raise their bridge hand off the cushion rail, so that they have only their fingertips touching, and at the same time address the cue ball with their back cueing hand raised, thus making a downward thrust at the cue ball (pictured). This is very wrong! The possibility of making a miscue is near certain because of the unsteady bridge hand. The awkward cue arm movement that will follow, and worse still, the fact that the player's head will be up off the cue guessing the potting angle instead of sighting it, all contribute to a bad shot. Now, because we are faced with an awkward lie and it is difficult, don't have any false ideas about it: we have to be firm with our approach to this particular lie, and above all we have to have confidence in our ability to handle these cushion shots because they appear quite regularly in games of snooker.

Firstly, chalk your tip, as always, for difficult shots. Secondly, place your bridge hand fingers to the outside edge of the cushion rail (little finger off cushion). Now with the bridge arm stretched out straight, and the bridge hand clamped to the cushion rail, we have a solid bridge and can concentrate on hitting the cue ball well because we can slide the cue back and forth with confidence. In making the stroke, the backward action is *slow* and *short*. The tip of the cue just brushes the edge of the cushion cloth before striking the cue ball. Do not allow the tip to run along the cushion cloth and raise the cue only slightly. This allows the player to have his normal stance and to get his head down over the cue for correct sighting.

Finally, never attempt to play a ball with speed from this position. The speed at which it is possible to play this shot with accuracy is at normal speed or even less. To attempt any more will result in a miscue or applying unintended spin. Recognize that you have a bad lie, and do not attempt anything difficult. By this I mean, put all your concentration into smooth central contact of the cue ball with the cue tip and getting the pot down. Do not make it even more difficult by trying to get perfect position at the same time, because the next shot will probably not be as difficult anyway.

27C – Awkward Bridging (Near the Cushion)

27C

With the cue ball 20 cm – 25 cm (8″ – 10″) out from the cushion, the 'clamp' bridge would be too far from the ball. This time the bridge is a little nearer the cue ball. We have fingers, palm and the base of the thumb all firmly on the cushion. With the palm flat on the cushion and with the fingers well spread, the cue slides along the channel formed by the knuckle of the forefinger and the thumb. This is not a grip. It is a channel for the cue to run in. Don't let the fingers tighten in on the cue. *Finally*, with this bridge, the cue should be as horizontal as possible, and with practice you can play with any speed you wish.

28A – Awkward Bridging (Over Balls)

The action being taken is bridging over balls. You can be confronted with this position at least once in each frame you may play.

Because I realize how easy it is to impart unintentional spin to the cue ball, I always keep in mind not to raise my cue higher than is necessary when clearing the obstructing ball or balls. Grip the cloth with the second, third and small finger pads firmly and allow the body weight to go onto these fingers. Tuck the forefinger up onto the second finger and cock the thumb as in the picture. I consider this is the best bridge possible, where the bridge hand can be put on to the table. It provides a firm bridge hand and allows the maximum height you may require with your bridge fingers, because you are not losing height trying to keep a shorter forefinger to the table.

28A

Points to note in the photograph: Firstly, that the fingers are well spread for strength and stability. Secondly, there is a great deal of pressure on the finger pads or rather the tips of the fingers. The fingers in fact are bending inwards under the pressure. The thumb is cocked even higher than usual. This adds to the height if extra height is required. A short slow backward action will help keep control. Again, do not attempt anything more than a moderately paced shot. If a higher bridge is required, raise the wrist, taking it more forward. This has the effect of bringing the little finger off the cloth, thus leaving two fingers of the tripod. This is a difficult shot. Take your time over placing the tripod fingers on the cloth. Having done so, brace the left arm out straight. When playing this shot, do not jab at the ball. And do not attempt to scoop at the ball. Confidence will come with practice.

28B – Awkward Bridging (Over Balls)

A position forcing me again to play over intervening balls. In this case the cue ball is not as close to the offending object balls as in the previous plate. I can comfortably get down to this shot by placing all four finger pads to the bed of the table with the arm going straight from the shoulder to the finger pads. Grip the cloth firmly with those four finger pads as you do not have the palm of the hand to carry your forward balance.

28B

29 – Bridging (Rest)

It is most important to get the head of the rest properly positioned. Most players place it too far away from the cue ball. The distance should not be more than 25 cm (10″). Having taken care to position the cross head on the table so as not to touch any ball, place the rest handle flat on the table, under the line of the cue, and clamp the handle down with the left hand.

Place your feet comfortably apart and square to the table. Body balance is forward through the straight left arm and onto the hand clamping the rest handle onto the table.

29

The grip of thumb and fingers on the butt is moderate, not over-firm and not too light. The flat on the butt of a cue is for the thumb to grip on, underneath the butt, and the first two fingers take their grip on top of the butt. Third and fourth fingers are bent and ride at the side of the butt. The *actual grip* is taken with thumb and first two fingers.

Butt of cue is slightly below level of chin and only raised as high as necessary to strike centrally. Elbow of cueing arm is at same level as butt of cue.

Cueing action is a backward push from the elbow, restricting the backswing to as short as 10 cm (4″). Follow through as far as possible and concentrate on striking the cue ball at 14.

30 – Bridging (Spider)

Using the spider is somewhat similar to the rest except that because the bridge of the spider is high a stroke is usually made downwards, with only the top of the cue ball to hit. Set yourself comfortably, as with the rest, and play into the ball. A point of importance to remember here is that because you are now playing down onto the cue ball, central vertical striking contact is very important. Striking of the cue tip down on to the cue ball, off the vertical centre line, will have a tendency to spear the cue ball off its course before reaching the object ball. If intending to follow through when using the object ball, striking point is 12 o'clock. If intending to stun

the cue ball to a stop, striking point is 14. To attempt a screw shot, the striking point is 6 o'clock. Be content with one of the advised striking positions on the cue ball. You are remaining on the vertical centre line of the cue ball, and will not be risking side on an already difficult shot.

30

31A – Follow Through (Straight Pot, Before)

This is a long, near straight pot to be followed through. Notice the cue tip addressing the cue ball at 12 o'clock. Struck here the cue ball will have top spin applied, the required spin essential for following through. The distance the cue ball will follow through the object ball will be determined by the power of the shot, strength of the stroke, or speed of the stroke, whichever way you like to look at it!

31A

31B

31B – Follow Through (Straight Pot, After)

Shows the completed follow through position. Having successfully made the shot, I have remained 'down' on the shot following the progress and resulting position of the cue ball, and only come up off the cue when the cue ball has come to rest.

Advanced Strokes for Break Building

Break building at snooker is one of the most enjoyable features of this game both for the player and the onlooker.

There is no great secret in being able to keep on potting when building breaks. It is simply a matter of potting with some consistency, positioning the cue ball to allow the next shot to be reasonably easy and, most important, to watch the lie of the object ball and to select the right ball to allow you to carry on the break. To make sizeable breaks regularly you must build up, in addition to some skill at potting, the essential strokes which will enable you to position on to the next ball. I consider the four main strokes in snooker to be the soft stun, the ordinary stun, the soft screw, and the deep screw. The importance of these four strokes for success at snooker is that they are employed stroke after stroke, for at least 90 per cent of my game.

Good players know the angles and paths of the object and cue balls automatically when playing the various shots in billiards and snooker. The learner must watch what is happening to his own strokes and also his opponent's strokes, in an endeavour to catch up to the better player. A good idea is to watch closely what is happening when a professional is playing a match, or better still, when a professional is practising. Notice the pace at which various shots are played, and pay close attention to where the cue ball is being struck by the cue tip, in potting and positional play. Most learners, for instance, are continually going in off, especially into the centre pockets. This is because their lack of angle knowledge, and ball path, lets them down.

Stun and Screw

In break building, many shots could be potted with plain central striking that would put the pot down, but would most assuredly put an end to the break, because you are not 'on' the next ball. Stun or screw gives much more control and once mastered, allows this shot to be played cleanly, crisply, and usually with enough power to keep the object ball on its straight path. Soft, dribbly shots are much too unreliable. Besides, conditions have to be perfect all the time to play this soft type of game, and there has only to be one small speck of dust or grit on the table for a ball's direction to be diverted.

Stun and screw shots can usually be employed in sending the object ball in with pace and at the same time checking your cue ball to the desired position. The difficult part of using these advanced strokes at snooker is the distinct possibility that the easiest of pots can be missed because of trying to get your cue ball in the most desired position. Even among leading professionals this continually happens.

The cause is the division of concentration. Besides having to put your pot down, you have also to move your cue ball, both in the direction you require and with the distance of travel you intend the cue ball to take in reaching your desired 'position'. Your first and foremost object is to put your pot down. This is much more important than missing the pot to get near-perfect position. By potting your ball you are retaining the strike, keeping your opponent away from the table, and most of all, you are continually building up your score, which is your ultimate aim.

Keep this point in mind: No matter how easy or how difficult a pot may appear, give it all the concentration it deserves.

Stun and screw strokes are for applying reverse spin to the cue ball. By striking the cue ball below centre at 15, you are applying reverse spin. Even though the cue ball goes forward, it is rotating backwards and, when the cue ball gets the impact of the object ball, its forward momentum is halted with a 'bounce-back' effect, and then the reverse spin gets a hold on the nap (cloth) and the ball comes back.

To apply spin to a cue ball effectively, certain conditions are necessary. Probably the most important of these is the tip of the cue itself. A hard, shiny tip will make the task of screwing back so much more difficult, simply because an 'overhard' tip cannot grip the cue ball and apply to it the intended 'twist'.

Balls will not respond to screw and stun if they are old and 'dead'. Balls, besides being chipped and cracked, can lose their resilience, and screw can be hard to impart on balls of unequal weights. Loss of resilience and unequal weights of balls are generally caused by old age.

The surface of a cloth also has quite an effect on a player's ability to play deep screw shots. The newer and heavier a cloth is, then the more it will take spin. A player probably could draw back further on a cloth of medium weight because the nap is fine and will let balls run on further than a heavy nap, but the heavy nap will take spin better.

I have mentioned the above-conditions before going onto the various ways of playing stun and screw shots, as I have had to play on poor conditions and I know that many players are forced to do the same. I know how hard screw and stun shots are to make successfully. Bad tables and balls can be a real headache, and besides this, I have watched the average player struggling to play these shots successfully with tips that are allowing him no chance of succeeding.

Perhaps a player can do nothing towards the reconditioning of a table, but every player can own his own cue, have a first-class tip on it, and can chalk the tip as regularly as is necessary to ensure no miscues.

A player has to keep in mind that if he intends to bring the cue ball back, then he has to hit low. *Most players do not do this.* They think they are striking the ball 'low', but their cue action is such that they actually strike the ball in the centre or just below centre, and they only stun the ball to a stop because the necessary back spin has not been applied for the screw shot.

Application of stun and screw, I consider, are the 'Shots of the Game'. I would like to request a closer study of my playing technique so that you, too, can learn to play these shots as confidently as I do. I am sure I can help all interested players with my explanations of these strokes.

42

Some of the reasons for 'lack of back spin' being achieved are as follows:

(a) Most players try to hit too hard, thus causing cueing errors, especially not getting their cue tip low to the ball.
(b) Striking too low, thus miscueing, or 'jumping' the cue ball.
(c) Instead of a controlled follow through for screw shots, too many employ a jerky, stabbing action that imparts no screw effect whatsoever.

There are many points concerning these strokes that I will cover later on, but to start with we will play all our stun and screw shots by striking 'low' and alternating the power and follow through to achieve our purpose.

Stance is of immense importance with these strokes. Where I normally have a bridge of 25 cm (10″) for plain central striking of the cue ball, I shorten my bridge to 20 cm (8″) for the stun and screw shots. Having moved my bridge hand closer to the cue ball to shorten the bridge, I now take a firmer grip of the cloth with the pads of my bridge hand fingers and a firmer grip of the cue with my cueing fingers. Because my bridge is shorter, my gripping position on the cue butt has also shortened up, so that the cueing forearm still hangs straight to the cue butt. The firmer grip of the bridge hand is for extra steadiness, and the firmer grip of the cueing hand is to feel the 'power', and 'grip of the tip', through to the cue ball.

For the screw shot, especially the deep screw, I have to play with some power. I have to be sure of striking as 'low' to the cue ball as I intend to. The firmer grip of bridge and cueing hand is to make my task easier. To strike the cue ball exactly where I intend to appears to be the easiest thing in the game, but in fact it is the hardest. Most amateurs play screw shots by striking too high. Result: no backspin has been applied. The fear of 'jumping' the ball or cutting the cloth is the main reason for players not striking low enough. Then there is the player who goes too 'low' and continually 'jumps' or miscues the cue ball. The place to strike the cue ball safely is midway between the centre of the cue ball and 6 o'clock. If you improve your cueing and continually strike here for your stun or screw shots, then all that remains to stun to a stop or screw back from 2.5 cm – 370 cm (1″ to 4 yards) is the power and 'feel' we impart through the cue, and the cue tip, to the cue ball.

To play these shots correctly the bridge hand must be lowered. Do this by turning the bridge hand over until the body weight is on to the base of the thumb, and the tip of the little finger barely reaches the cloth. This, in effect, lowers the groove between thumb and forefinger in which the cue runs. The bridge hand grip is firm. Having lowered the tip to the cue ball by lowering the bridge hand, the next step is to lower the cue hand, so that the whole cue is down and horizontally level. Do not play downward strokes when addressing the bottom of the cue ball for screw shots – you have to play straight into the ball.

The action for stun-screw is shorter than the normal back stroke. The forward stroke is also shorter than normal, because of our 'shortened-up' stance. The distance of my follow through on a screw shot is 8 cm (3″). On impact with the cue ball, I take a distinctly stronger hold on the cue without checking the action. This applies the 'bite'. It is the prolonged grip of the tip on the cue ball, plus the bite of the stroke itself, that creates the backspin.

Feel the screw as you apply it, from your cue hand, through the cue, to the tip onto and into the ball. Do not swing through the ball, but strike it with a crisp, clean stroke. The difference between screwing back 30 cm (12″) and the length of the table is only the power put into the shot.

The two main obstacles against playing screw shots successfully are the distance between cue ball and object ball, and the thickness of contact when putting the pot down.

1. The further the balls are apart, the more power has to be applied to keep backspin on the cue ball till it reaches the object ball.
2. For the cue ball to be screwed back, contact of cue ball onto object ball has to be thick. Contact of less than half ball is not enough to get the cue ball anywhere but across the table after contact. I can alter the pull of the cue ball after thin contact on the object ball, but only slightly, by adding side to the screw. This, of course, makes the pot harder to get, and unless a player is advanced with his cueing, it is without doubt one of the hardest strokes to play in the game.

When attempting a screw shot, consider the distance between the cue ball and your 'target' ball, and look closely at the angle of your pot so that you know if contact will be thick enough to allow a screw back to be played.

To check over the main points for screw shots again:

(a) Make sure of the pot.
(b) Screw is reverse spin.
(c) A firm tip is ideal.
(d) Make sure of striking low.
(e) Stance to be firmer than normally.
(f) Lower the tip, and the butt, of the cue.
(g) The cue action is shorter, with a snappy, striking movement, tightening the grip on impact.

When first learning to screw back, make straight pots so that you are playing full onto the object ball with the cue ball. Commence your practice by playing with just enough power to pull the cue ball back several inches from a distance of 30 cm (12″). Add power gradually until you can pull back several feet.

Remember, before you can hope to screw back the length of the table, you have to learn first to screw back half the length of the table, then by adding to the power of your stroke, screw back a little further each time till you can screw back 370 cm (12′) or more. It is very rarely that one wishes to screw the cue ball back any further than 370 cm (12′).

32A, B – Stun (Straight Through)

With the cue ball and object ball being left in a similar position, this time the desired positioning of the cue ball was to travel forward only half the distance as the previous follow through because, in this instance, the black was further down the table. This shot is played with added power to the last shot (31A), again allowing the cue to go through. Striking point on the cue ball now, however, is 14. (Plate A shows shot before being played, Plate B shows result.)

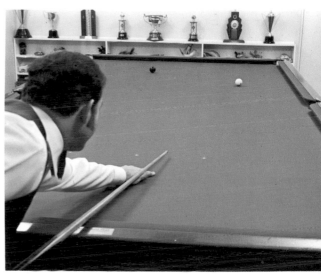

32A

32B

33A, B – Stun (Angle Pot)

This shot is played with the same power as the stun through (32). Now, however, there is to be no follow through with the cue arm. I stop my cue on striking the cue ball by taking hold of the cue on impact. By closing my cue hand firmer on the cue at impact with the cue ball, it provides a 'deadener' on the cue ball. *Stop your cue arm on impact, as well.* Striking point on the cue ball – 15. (Plate A shows shot before being played, Plate B shows result.)

33A

33B

34 – Stun (Angle Across)

Shows an angle to the intended pot. Now because cue ball contact on to the object ball is approximately a half ball contact, I cannot expect to stun straight through, or hold, without sacrificing the pot by striking the object ball too full.

The pocketing of the object ball is first and foremost. The contact must be half ball. In playing position, however, there are several lines away to the right of the object ball that I can dictate the cue ball to follow.

The line will be determined by my striking point of cue tip on to cue ball, and the strength I put into the stroke.

I ask you to study this plate seeing:

1. The red line of the object ball to the intended pocket.
2. The white lines of the cue ball away on just three lines that could be used in gaining your desired position.

Striking point on the cue ball to follow: – line (a) would be 15; line (b) would be 6 o'clock; and line (c) would also be 6 o'clock. Note here the different direction acquired from line (b) to line (c) when both shots were played at 6 o'clock to the cue ball. The reason for the change of angle away from the red ball is also the reason for the extra travel of cue ball (c). The shot was played with added power. My intention on the first two shots (in the stun family) was to hold for the pink, the third shot my intention was to position on the blue for the centre pocket. I will deal with this technique more fully in Practice later on.

35 – Screw (Back)

The required essentials here are to chalk your cue carefully; address the cue ball at 6 o'clock; take a firmer grip than normal with your bridge and cue hands; shorten your bridge to 20 cm (8″), at the same time shortening your gripping point with your cue hand to suit; play your stroke with a smooth, controlled, rhythmic drive, delivering your cue into and through the cue ball, with as much follow through as possible, without moving forward, off balance.

36 – Screw (Back with Side)

Here is a straight pot on the black. I intend not only to screw back to the side cushion in front of me, but to send the cue ball down the table to split the two reds.

To screw back without side, in potting the black, my cue ball would not reach the two reds (as indicated by white line (a), after striking the cue ball at 6 o'clock, and contacting the black full, ensuring the pot).

To move the cue ball further to my right, from the cushion in front of me, from white line (a) to white line (b), thus ensuring the splitting of the two reds, *side* has to be applied as well as backspin.

To move my cue ball to my right, after it comes back to the cushion from the black ball, the cue ball must be struck on the left. Low to bring it back from the black ball, left to make it pull to the right on reaching the cushion. Therefore, striking point on the cue ball, 7 o'clock.

In striking the cue ball at 7 o'clock, and at the desired speed to make sure the cue ball gets into the reds with enough power to split them open, allowance has to be made in your aiming onto the black ball. I will explain how and why in my next chapter on The Effects of Side, but in Plate 36 I ask you to note a second black ball placed against the cushion, and near to the intended corner pocket.

I have placed the second black ball there to indicate to you that I am aiming the cue ball at the black on its spot to the position the second black is occupying near the corner pocket. When I strike the cue ball at 7 o'clock and at the speed I intend to, I will make the black right into the pocket! You wonder why? The reason is that when I strike the cue ball low and left at 7 o'clock, the force of my cue going into the cue ball will force it away to the right of my intended aiming point on the black. This, in turn, will send the black not to the second black, but to the pocket. Just as well I allowed for this movement of the cue ball, in my aim!

37 – Screw (Deep)

To be played exactly as the screw back shown and explained in Plate 36. *Remember*, however, to increase the distance you intend to bring the cue ball back, by applying backspin, striking point on the cue ball must be 6 o'clock, and added power from the cue arm determines the distance of the cue ball travel.

37

38A, B – Screw (Black to Yellow)

Two shots often called for in top snooker, in gaining best position on yellow, before taking all the colours. Line (a) away from black, direct to the desired position, without touching a cushion will be achieved by striking cue ball at 5 o'clock. Line (b) using one cushion to the desired position will be achieved by striking cue ball at 7 o'clock with added power. Cue ball movement to black will have to be allowed for in aiming in both cases.

38A, B

49

Side

The use of side can be a source of great satisfaction and accomplishment. However, I am bound to warn you that it could create trouble, so my advice to players in the early stages of learning to play snooker is *'don't use side'*.

When a player becomes good enough to control his cue action really well, then by all means let him use side, but only then when it is really necessary. Even then, use it when the cue ball has only a short distance to travel to the object ball. Using side on long shots is extremely dangerous. Some professionals; as well as amateurs of all grades, use side on the cue ball when it has to travel the length of the table before making its first contact. These shots are so uncertain that mostly, when they succeed, it is just through luck. The amount of allowance to be estimated, in making these side shots of push off and swerve back of the cue ball in playing soft, medium or power shots, is nothing more than a rough guess.

What does happen when we apply side? Most people think that when they hit the cue ball on the right side, it will immediately start curving away to the right! This is not the case. The first bite of the cue tip into the right side of the cue ball will push it out to the left until the initial impetus is spent and then the right hand side exerts itself and pulls the ball to the right. This, in fact, means that when the ball has side (spin) applied to it, a curve takes place which is subject to all sorts of fluctuations and degrees. The effect of side is created by the nap of cloth: the heavier the nap, the more spin effect.

Yet another factor is the speed at which the stroke is played: the more power that is applied when using side, the longer the travel of the cue ball will be before curving back after the push-off is exhausted.

If the distance between the cue ball and object ball is four feet, the cue ball, with right hand side applied, at less than medium pace, would have time to recover from being pushed out to the left and would move off its line to the right. Some allowance would therefore have to be made for this movement when sighting. Playing the same stroke with power would mean that the cue ball would hardly have recovered from its push-off to left, created by the impact of the cue tip to the right side of the ball, by the time it reached the object ball. Texture of the nap will affect these calculations, as will variations in the weather. Slackness of the cloth will affect the grip of a spinning ball. More especially, there is a difference when using side (spin) with and against the nap.

You will now appreciate the complications of using side. I use it only when positively necessary, and I hope to convince you also to play the game safely, as I do.

Previously I have written on the importance of stroking your cue on a horizontal plane, and when applying side to the cue ball, this is more important than for most shots.

When using side on the cue ball for a close shot, allowance must be made for the amount of 'push-off' when aiming. When the cue ball and the object ball are further apart, allowance for swing back must be made in aiming. The amount of 'push-off' and 'swing back' can only be regulated by the power of the stroke and by the amount of *side imparted*. If the side is weak, the cue tip strikes the cue ball just off centre, but if it is strong, it will strike the cue ball well out to the side.

To get an understanding of the amount of 'push-off' or 'swing back' when applying side, place the black ball on its spot and the cue ball 46 cm (18″) from the black so that the pot is not straight, but there is a half ball contact to pot the black ball in the right hand pocket at the black spot end. This would make the black a straight pot to the top cushion, approximately 61 cm (24″) back from the centre of the pocket. This now means that right hand side applied to the cue ball will be 'running' side and the left hand side will 'check' the cue ball.

For this test of 'push-off' we will use *right* side. Aim to pot the black, striking the cue ball midway between the centre of the ball and the right edge. Use sufficient power to make the cue ball travel to the top cushion and down to the centre pocket after black ball contact on a table of average speed. The cue ball will strike the side cushion approximately 15 cm (6″) above the right centre pocket. However, if you have been aiming to pot the black ball into the middle of the top right hand pocket and have actually struck the cue ball midway between its centre and the right edge with enough power for the cue ball to reach the centre pocket, you will have missed by several inches to the right of the pocket on the side cushion. This is because you pushed the cue ball away from the cue tip to the left, overcutting the black ball when the cue ball travelled its 46 cm (18″) to the black. Allowance should have been made for push off in aiming to pot the black when using the right hand side.

Remember: The more power used the greater the 'push-off'. A soft stroke will generate practically no 'push-off' at all.

Combining *side with screw* is often very useful, but it is certainly going to complicate the shot and add to the possibility of the shot going wrong.

Only a very good cueist can add side to a screw shot with any degree of consistent success. Cueing has to be confident, and positively first class. This is a shot where one has to have the knowledge of what will happen when:

(a)   The cue tip strikes the cue ball, softly, moderately, or with drive.

(b)   Side is used sparingly, moderately or excessively.

For a thorough understanding of what is going to happen when strokes combining side and screw are employed, when these strokes should be used, and how much side and screw to use, my advice to any learner (and for that matter, most experienced players) is to have a private lesson from a professional player, as there are many items to be understood which I cannot explain here because of limited space.

From the safety angle, the best way to use screw is the plain straightforward stroke, with a smooth follow through, using a very firm grip. Professional players vary in their methods of achieving a given amount of screw, depending on their touch, technique and skill. A learner's degree of application will also vary as he improves so that, when he can screw back 30 cm (12″) when 38 cm (15″) from the object ball and playing his stroke at a certain speed and hitting his cue ball at a certain depth, he will find that, as his timing and technique improve, the cue ball will come back a little further all the time.

Practise your cue shots this way: Place the balls 30 cm (12″) apart and play a medium pace full ball screw back. Note the distance the cue ball comes back. Play continuously at that distance, steadily increasing the power until you have doubled and trebled the distance of screw back. Do not let your aim slip. Make certain you are potting your ball.

You must allow for the effect of the nap when making shots using side. The nap runs from the baulk end to the spot end of the table. There are thousands of threads from the baulk end to the spot (top) end, each made up of a mass of tiny fibres fitting into and overlapping each other like scales on a fish.

This nap affects all medium and slow strokes with and against the lay of the nap, but has very little effect across the nap.

In fast or power strokes, the pace of the stroke discounts nap effect. In slow or medium paced strokes, the nap, when applying side (spin), exercises strong influence. The effect of side up the table (with the nap) increases in proportion as the ball slows down.

With medium and slow strokes against the nap it will take effect in a contrary way. Instead of the cue ball spinning away to the right, when struck on the right side by the cue tip, it turns to the *left*. Across the table, the side and nap effect on straight shots is practically non-existent. In diagonal and slow shots, it does operate to some extent.

With and against the nap it is the pulling away tendency of the cue ball that we have to take into account, and as we know, the pull is in a different direction with the nap than against it.

To run through the object ball and expect the cue ball on reaching a cushion to pull to the right, then the cue ball should be struck high on the right side (1 o'clock). To screw back and expect the cue ball to pull to the right after contact with a cushion, the cue ball should be hit low on the left side (7 o'clock) – the opposite to going forward.

39 –Side (Left, Run Through Black)

Here is a position often attained while playing snooker. I am nicely on the black ball and I intend to run through the black to the top cushion, side cushion, out around and nicely behind the red ball.

39

Red line indicates path of black to pocket. White line indicates intended path of the cue ball and the three cue balls show the stroke, point of contact and finishing position. Striking point of cue tip to cue ball will be 2 o'clock. (Some top to make cue ball run, combined with right spin to pull cue ball around the two cushions, on the intended line.)

A smooth follow through of the cue is essential. Let the cue follow through after impact onto the cue ball. Aim on to black ball has to allow for movement of the cue ball, on its journey to the black ball. The speed of stroke to be used in gaining desired position will determine the amount of 'push-off' of cue ball to black ball. In turn this governs the distance from pocket the black ball is to be aimed at to allow for that 'push-off'. White mark on cushion indicates position I will aim black to. After 'push-off' has taken place, correct contact onto the black ball as indicated by the second cue ball will result in the black following the intended line to pocket.

40 – Side (Check Against Running)

Shows exactly the same position on the black ball. The intention on this occasion is to firstly pot the black, and in doing so, to check the cue ball off the top cushion only, for desired position on the red ball. From this position check side will be left side – striking point on cue ball, 10 o'clock.

Smooth follow through is again essential, strength of stroke important, and applying opposite spin, as compared to last shot, means aiming allowance on to black ball will be opposite to spin previously used. Note white mark on cushion, adjacent to pocket, black ball is to be aimed at.

40

41 – Side (Soft Shot)

41

Both previous shots have had to be played with medium-paced strength, and allowance has had to be made for movement away from cue tip of cue ball. Plate 41 shows a shot set up where again side is to be applied to the cue ball. The strength now intended for positioning the cue ball is going to be soft.

Playing into the cue ball with right hand side, with a smooth follow through, at slow speed and with more of a push than a stroke, very little 'push-off' of cue ball from cue tip is going to take place. As the right spin (striking point on cue ball – 3 o'clock) is going to be strong, however, aim on to black ball will have to be the same as the last shot, but for a different reason. Now the spinning cue ball will affect the black object ball.

The applied right spin on a soft shot will 'throw' the object ball the opposite way – *left*, always, provided the cue ball is struck on the right with sufficient strength for spin still to be active on cue ball when it reaches black ball. On Plate 41 my aiming point on the black ball is to send it to the white mark on the far side pocket jaw (as indicated). The spin from the cue ball *(right)* will *not* transfer to the black ball – but will throw the black ball the opposite way – to the left – and thus into the pocket along correct path as indicated.

42 – Side (Power Shot)

42

The same shot as the previous one, using the same intended side on the cue ball.

In this instance, however, the shot is to be played with power to force the cue ball around the angles and down the table. The striking point on the cue ball is going to be the same as shown and described in Plate 41. In this case, however, the black ball is aimed to the white mark shown on the opposite side of the pocket. Whereas on the soft shot (Plate 41) I had to allow for the spinning cue ball throwing the black object ball. In this case, because power is required, I must make allowance for the cue ball being pushed away from the cue tip. Cue ball and object ball will follow the paths as shown.

Practice

To improve your snooker, you must practise. Then for your practice to be beneficial to you, it should be carried out regularly and along correct lines.

When about to practise, do not worry about finding an opponent. Playing with an opponent all the time may keep you in form, but practising along sound lines by yourself will bring more rapid improvement.

Two players setting about to play a frame of snooker together, especially when learning the game, do not realize how difficult they are making it for each other to improve their game. What usually happens is that the first player breaks the reds and only three or four come out, and he has the cue ball back in baulk. Unless one red has found its way over a pocket, his opponent has been left a reasonably hard shot to try and score. So both players have not much chance of scoring on their opening strokes. After several shots, one usually sees five reds still jammed together with the five or six remaining reds hard against the cushions. Not very good conditions for learning to pot or learning to position the cue ball. To make matters even worse, several colours may also be against the cushions, because following potted reds the colours have been missed and are off their spots. Nobody can go on potting hard balls.

A champion at snooker undoubtedly has the ability to work the cue ball around the table in making good position, thus making each following pot easy. This is the main reason for big breaks. In Australia today there are hundreds of good potters but there are few champions at snooker. The main reason, I consider, is that very few players practise correctly and sufficiently long enough to become proficient at sighting, cueing and touch. Then again, it is no good being a sound position player if you are missing your pots. We must learn to pot first.

43A – Practice (Plain White Only, Centre Spots)

Learn to groom accurate cueing:

(a)   Place cue ball on brown spot.
(b)   Aim to fire cue ball over pink spot.
(c)   Strike cue ball dead centre, 14.
(d)   Strike with sufficient power to return over brown spot.

If cue ball returns over brown spot, then cueing has been perfect. If cue ball returns to right or left of brown spot after passing over pink spot on way up table, the cueing has been bad. If cue ball pulls to right or left after striking top cushion, left or right hand side has been applied. Keep practising until cue ball travels up and down table over the spots, shot after shot.

43B – Practice (Plain White Only, Left and Right Baulk)

This exercise is to apply and control side (spin).

(a) Place cue ball on brown spot.
(b) Aim to fire cue ball over pink spot.
(c) Strike cue ball 3 o'clock (to pull to right), 9 o'clock (to pull to left).
(d) Strike with sufficient power to strike side cushions (where baulk line meets cushions).

Smooth, groomed cueing will ensure the cue ball will travel over pink spot on way to top cushion. Applied spin then pulling cue ball to where baulk line meets cushions. If cue ball is struck at 3 o'clock (pull to right) or 9 o'clock (pull to left) and does not pull out to fulfil ultimate aim, shot has probably not been played with enough power, therefore spin has gone from cue ball, by the time it has reached the top cushion.

43C – Practice (Plain White Only, Above Centre Pockets, Left and Right, Excessive Side)

This practice exercise is similar to Plate 43B. However, to pull cue ball acutely enough to reach side cushions above centre pockets, more power is essential. Apply added power to this shot, strike cue ball at 5 o'clock (pull to right) and 7 o'clock (pull to left) to achieve your object. Again true, groomed, fluent cueing is a must. Chalk tip well for these shots and keep cue as horizontally level as possible.

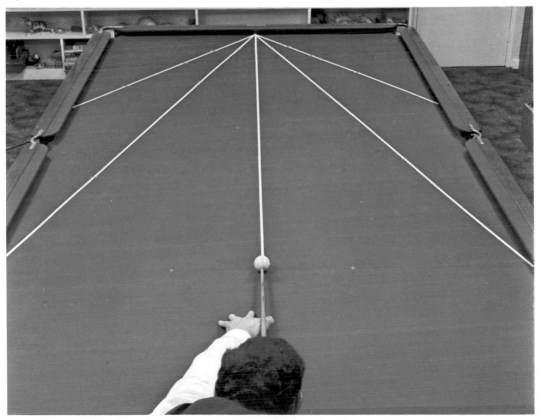

44 – Practice (Long Straight Pot)

A long, straight pot – probably my favourite practice technique for perfect cueing. Gather all 21 object balls into a corner of the baulk area of the table. Place one ball at a time halfway down the table (as shown), then position cue ball on the baulk line in a position setting the object ball up for a straight pot into the top corner pocket. You are setting out to pot all 21 object balls, one at a time, in this exercise. Vary the position of the object ball between the blue spot and the centre pockets so that you get an opportunity of playing the cue ball fully across the baulk line. You only need to play from off the baulk line the width of the 'D'.

To continually pocket this long, straight pot, your stance, aim and cueing will have to be perfect as you will not make the shot if any of those three vital fundamentals are not working correctly. On setting your stance and aligning your cue to play full on to the red ball, do not sight at the pocket, as you can see the pocket in the background. Your sighting concentration, at the time of delivering the stroke, should be on the red.

Strike the cue ball at point 15 intending to stun the cue ball at position where cue ball contacts object ball. Weight forward on to bridge arm and bridge hand. Rear leg remains straight, left knee bent with slightly more weight on the left foot than the right. A smooth, well groomed and fluent stroke is essential. Strike with a brisk action to stun the cue ball dead on contacting the object ball. Try to practise this type of shot for one hour each day.

45A

45A – Practice (Blue Only, Various Positions)

Blue to pink from below left: In practising this shot, which often occurs in snooker, the cue ball, in following the intended line, must have left spin applied checking cue ball against running on to side cushion. Aiming point on to blue is on the 'thickish' side to send blue to white mark indicated on the pocket jaw. The cue ball at address is to be struck at 10 o'clock. Left hand spin being applied to the cue ball will throw the blue to the centre of the pocket. Correct strength of stroke is essential. Ideal position on pink is achieved by use of only one cushion (top cushion) as shown.

45B – Practice (Blue Only, Various Positions)

Blue to pink from below left: From this position, centre ball striking (12 o'clock) on the cue ball allows sighting on to blue to centre of middle pocket (no spin effect). Desired path of cue ball from this natural angle will be off two cushions for ideal position.

45B

45C

45C – Practice (Blue Only, Various Positions)

Blue to pink from below left: Again 12 o'clock striking of the cue ball on to blue (aimed to centre of middle pocket) will result in the cue ball following a shorter, direct path to same desired position.

45D, E, F – Practice (Blue Only, Various Positions)

Blue to pink below right: These three shots from similar positions on the opposite side of the table are to be played the same way, except that on Plate 45A striking point now is 2 o'clock instead of 10 o'clock.

45D, E, F

46A – Practice (Pink Only, From Bottom Left to Corner Pocket)

From nearest cue ball, aim to pocket pink ball to the centre of the pocket with sufficient power to position cue ball along indicated path. Striking point on the cue ball, 15. Clip the cue ball cleanly with a brisk stroke.

46B – Practice (Pink Only, From Bottom Left to Corner Pocket)

From second cue ball (off straight), aim pink ball to centre of pocket. Striking point on cue ball, 12 o'clock. Play with sufficient strength for cue ball to travel indicated path to side cushion and off to point shown.

46B

46C – Practice (Pink Only, From Bottom Left to Corner Pocket)

From third cue ball, aim to overcut pink to white mark on top cushion. Strike cue ball at 5 o'clock with power for cue ball to follow intended path to Point C. The drive of the cue tip at 5 o'clock on the cue ball will automatically push cue ball thicker into pink ball than aim intended, because of the power used, taking pink ball cleanly into pocket.

46C

46D, E, F —Practice
(Pink Only, From Bottom Right to Corner Pocket)

These three shots from similar positions on the opposite side of the table are to be played the same way as Plate 46C, except that striking point now is 7 o'clock instead of 5 o'clock.

46D, E, F

47A – Practice (Pink Only, From Above Left to Middle Pocket)

From cue ball, aim pink ball to centre of middle pocket along intended path shown. Strike cue ball at 12 o'clock with a smooth follow through action that will allow the cue ball to travel the intended path. Some power is required for this shot.

47B – Practice (Pink Only, From Above Left to Middle Pocket)

From cue ball aim pink ball to centre of middle pocket, striking cue ball below centre at 15. This is a stun shot to force cue ball to travel intended path to point for position on black ball at opposite side of table. To apply stun effect to the cue ball (*no* follow through of the cue ball), stop the cue on striking cue ball.

47B

47C – Practice (Pink Only, From Above Left to Middle Pocket)

From cue ball (near straight pot position), aim pink ball to centre of middle pocket. Strike cue ball at 6 o'clock. Screw back on same line from pink ball back to ideal position on black ball.

47C

47D, E, F —Practice
(Pink Only, From Above Right to Middle Pocket)

These three shots from similar positions on the opposite side of the table are to be played the same way.

All these shots in the 47 group are ones I consistently play, because on each occasion I can get from pink ball to black ball without applying side spin on any of the six shots employed. I have continued to strike with vertical centre striking on the cue ball, as I advocate for most pot shots in the game.

47D, E, F

48A, B, C, D – **Practice (Pot Black 200 Times)**

Over the years I have spent many hours on this special practice technique of potting the black off its spot from the position shown 200 times. The position of the cue ball is not the position to keep coming back to, it is merely the commencing position. The exercise combines positional play with potting. Therefore, after each pot, you should be leaving yourself in the desired position for your next shot.

The four shots indicated on Plate 48 are four shots that can be played in the following order and are just four of my favourite ways of keeping the cue ball back on to the black:

1. Plate 48A. Aim black ball to centre of the pocket shown by red line. Cue ball to follow path of line to point shown. Striking point on cue ball 12 o'clock. Correct strength of stroke is very important.
2. Plate 48B. Aim black to centre of the pocket. Striking point on cue ball 13, for intended travel of cue ball to point shown. Strength of stroke again important.

48A

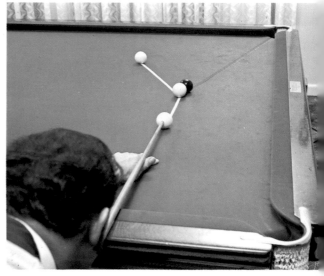

48B

3. Plate 48C. Aim black to centre of the pocket. Striking point of cue ball 12 o'clock, again with sufficient strength for the cue ball to follow intended path travelling two cushions to point shown.

4. Plate 48D. Aim black to centre of the pocket. Striking point on cue ball 15, with sufficient strength for cue ball to follow intended path to point shown.

These are four potting and positional shots, played in sequence on the black, always aiming the cue ball on to the black to centre of corner pocket without any side spin (left or right) ever being applied to cue ball. If you repeat these moves, along with quite a few other positioning shots, you are well on the way to potting the black ball the 200 intended times. What better practice than this for becoming proficient at potting the black from off its spot?

48C

48D

49

Place the 21 object balls, spread out, all over the table. Keep them out from the cushions and apart, keeping in mind that this is to be straight-out potting. Do not worry about getting a red then a colour. Pot anything. The idea is that because there are six pockets on the table and 21 balls to be potted, you are getting a pot at each pocket, and practically every shot you play will be a different angle.

You set yourself the task of trying to pot the 21 shots. When you can do this, you have become proficient at the first stage of snooker. You are learning to pot as the champions do. If at first you find that you have taken, say, 40 or 50 shots to put the lot down, count your misses, set them up again and try to beat your last score. You will see that when you make your first pot there are several reds to choose from, but as you thin them out, you have also to pay more attention to positional play. In practising this 21 ball technique from the start, play reasonable position by at least concentrating on keeping the cue ball out from cushions. You should never finish with the cue ball against a cushion. Place the cue ball anywhere to start, keep concentrating, and keep at it.

50

This is a practice technique that I have used since my early playing days on advice I received as a schoolboy from the late and great Walter Lindrum. It is marvellous practice for learning the potting angle and adding cue ball control at the same time.

The task I set myself here, and advise you to adopt, is to line all 21 object balls down the centre of the table; you should fit them between the brown and pink spots. Use your cue to pull them into a reasonably good line, and put cue ball into a handy position to start. The task you are setting yourself all the time is to take all 21 object balls, without a miss, and to do so without the cue ball ever touching the cushions.

Again we apply the three important points I have previously outlined to you:

1. The potting of the object ball.
2. The correct striking of cue tip on to cue ball.
3. The feel of your cue, as to how hard or how soft to play each shot for a gaining position.

Place the cue ball into a handy position to start, making an angle to the first pot.

71

First and foremost, all the time, pocket the object ball. This is plain, straight out good sighting judgement backed up, of course, with a good cue action.

Positioning the cue ball around the table is a combination of two things:

(a) Where you strike the cue ball with the tip of your cue which will dictate to the cue ball the angle you want it to come away from the object ball on; and

(b) The strength of the stroke, which will further determine how far the cue ball is going to travel along the intended line.

In setting out to take all 21 object balls without a miss and without the cue ball ever touching the cushion, I have to look ahead. I unfailingly pocket all 21 object balls without a miss, time after time. Yet when I set out to clear the balls again, I never set out looking 21 shots ahead, as I have no set technique in taking the 21 object balls; I will, however, look ahead at least as far as this shot and the next: what am I going to pocket now, what area am I going to move the cue ball into, and what is my next shot going to be?

To regularly and consistently carry out this exercise, I make an angle on my next shot each time. It is the angle that I make on each object ball that enables me to work up and down the line without ever touching the cushions. If I make a straight pot, I can only run through that pot to the other side of the table or I can only draw back. When commencing this practice technique, however, you will soon find out that you cannot work from the extreme ends of the balls if you are making straight pots. You must create an angle to your pots to be able to carry out the exercises and I make an angle that allows me to pull the cue ball away from the line of balls and not risk the problem of having my cue ball kissing, and getting caught up in, the line of balls.

In practising this marvellous technique for potting, positioning and developing touch, do not run the cue ball through or draw it back too far, leaving too much distance between the line of balls or running the risk of getting the cue ball back near a cushion. At the same time, do not under-hit your shots leaving the cue ball too close into the balls as, from a position like that, you will find that there are no balls on because you could not play them past one another, for the corner pockets in particular. Concentrate on keeping the cue ball a comfortable distance from the line of balls and no further back than say, halfway between the line of balls and the side cushion.

51 – Practice (Advance Line Up)

Now you see the colours on their correct spots. The line of reds are spaced in as follows: 1 above the black ball, 5 between black and pink balls, 7 between pink and blue balls, and 2 below the blue ball. We are now moving into the break building family of practice techniques.

Always set out from the position shown to make a 100 break or clear the table.

After each red, you must take a colour, after a colour back to the next red. I have passed 1,300 century breaks at snooker to this stage of my career. This is one of the practice techniques that has meant so much to me in acquiring my break building skill in matches at snooker. I have practised this advanced line up for hours and hours and hours during my career, always striving for accuracy in my potting and cue ball control by correct striking on to the areas of the cue ball called for in the 36 shots that I will have to play if I am to clear the table. I am working always to perfect my strength of stroke, for each and every shot will at times call for soft, medium and power strokes.

Again I have no set technique on how I will take the balls. I run the cue ball around cushions, across the table, down the table and up the table in my relentless pursuit of at least 100 break. I always count my break as it builds up, as I find this helps my concentration immensely, particularly in my big matches. When playing before an audience of 2,000 people, compiling a big break when I am concentrating correctly is little different, in fact, to compiling a big break in my own billiard room on my own, practising.

Try to keep clear of cushions. Do not get too close to the line of balls – always work to keep your cue ball clear of the line of balls. I realize that you would never see a situation in a game of snooker where the balls would come out as they are positioned now, however I have purposely placed the balls where they are so all the balls can be taken, providing my potting and positional play is good. This technique is tremendous for acquiring the skill that is needed to make big breaks in actual games at Club level, or even in Championship matches.

51

52

A second break building situation that I often use continually to perfect my break building technique. Again, as in Plate 51, set off by taking a red, a colour, a red, a colour, etc., always striving to clear the table or make a 100 break at least. Dedication with this type of practice will increase your potting ability and knowledge of positional play. Keep working hard at this technique and improvement is sure to come.

53A –Practice (Colours from Spots)

The picture shows the ideal position of cue ball to commence taking all six colours. Aim yellow ball to the centre of the pocket. Strike cue ball dead centre at 14. The desired strength is for cue ball to follow indicated path, finishing nicely on green.

53B –Practice (Colours from Spots)

Aim green to centre of pocket. Strike cue ball at 6 o'clock drawing cue ball directly off green to several inches outside of baulk line along intended path, to point shown. On striking cue ball, stop delivery of cue as for stun shot.

53C –Practice (Colours from Spots)

Aim brown ball to centre of pocket. Strike cue ball, below centre at 15 to follow intended path to side cushion and off to a point for perfect position on blue ball. This shot definitely has to be played at the right speed as finishing short will leave a difficult shot on the blue in attaining ideal position on the pink ball. The same will apply if the shot from brown ball is over-hit, resulting in cue ball travelling beyond the desired point. No side is required for this shot. The angle on cue ball to brown ball in making the pot is a natural angle when cue ball struck at 15.

53C

53D

53D –Practice (Colours from Spots)

Aim blue to centre of pocket. Striking point on cue ball, above centre at 13. A soft, smooth stroke will result in the cue ball following intended path from blue to a point shown for a near straight pink ball.

76

53E – Practice (Colours from Spots)

Aim pink ball to centre of pocket. Striking point on cue ball, above centre at 12 o'clock. A smooth follow through with your cue action with the right strength of stroke to follow through pink ball for good position on black ball.

53E

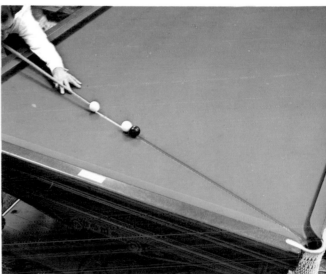

53F

53F – Practice (Colours from Spots)

Pot Black! Aim black ball to centre of the pocket. Strike cue ball below centre at 15 stunning cue ball to a dead stop at point of contact, as shown. Remain steady and cue carefully in making certain of potting the black. Irrespective of how easy it looks this should get the full concentration that every shot in snooker deserves. I have seen this simple looking shot missed on many occasions by top players, as well as learners, simply because the shot is taken for granted.

This series of shots (53A to F) was a perfect way of clearing the table by taking all 6 colours. Having played a good shot by getting the cue ball into the desired opening position on the yellow, it is not difficult to take the remaining five coloureds, providing you do not shun your practice. I would hope that you have noticed that, by playing snooker the Eddie Charlton way, never once has your cue tip been away from the vertical centre line of the cue ball. That has to be good snooker!

Doubling

An experienced player often recognizes that a scoring stroke can be made from a ball tucked up on a cushion, a stroke that would go unnoticed by an inexperienced player. The experienced player realizes that a ball can be doubled on to cushions, and around angles, in making scoring strokes.

On doubling, my technique in attempting a scoring shot, is to use only one cushion in preference to two, two cushions in preference to three, three cushions in preference to four, and so on, and never with excessive power.

Doubling is difficult even to the most experienced players. I attempt doubles always at a speed that will bring the object ball away from the intended pocket area, should I miss. In effect I attempt doubling on the basis that it is a shot to nothing, as I will have reasonable safety should I miss the shot. Any player attempting doubles has the odds against him, therefore I always consider the situation carefully before attempting the double, in case a safety shot may be in my better interests.

However there are occasions when a game can be won by doubling a ball by use of the cushions. I rarely double without the distinct possibility of being able to play a sound position shot to carry on with. In attempting doubles, do not play with any more power than you think is necessary, as a very common fault by most players is to force the object ball into a cushion at excessive speed. What invariably happens is that the ball, having been buried into the rubber cushion with no side applied to it in going on to the cushion, will have spin applied to it when it comes off. Having been thrown off the rubber cushion at speed and depending at which angle, that spin will react from the next cushion that it goes to, should more than one cushion be attempted. Most snooker players can never understand, when attempting a double across the table to a middle pocket, why the ball off the second cushion will straighten up and then spend the rest of its journey travelling backwards and forwards across the table instead of taking the angle the player was looking for.

Probably the main problem with doubling is finding the correct angle to the pocket. Try and keep in mind that a ball at slow to medium pace speeds with no spin applied to it, will come off a cushion on the same line of angle that it went on. Therefore, in assessing the line of the object ball to the pocket, you should be looking for the line of the red on to the cushion and from that point of the cushion to the pocket.

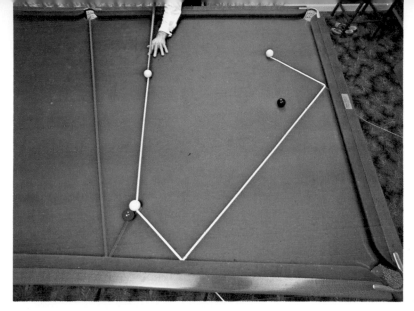

54A

54A –Doubling (Single Ball, Off One Side Cushion)

Sight the line of the red ball to the cushion, allowing for it to come off the cushion on the same line to the intended pocket. Strike the cue ball at 13 to pass around the black ball, on intended line, for the black ball next shot. The strength that you have played the shot in acquiring cue ball to the indicated position is of sufficient strength for red ball to be clear of the intended middle pocket at that speed.

54B –Doubling (Single Ball, Off One Side Cushion)

We see a red ball close to the middle pocket but not on for that centre pocket for a direct shot because of the narrow opening at that angle. Cue ball is now into the desired position for making one of the simple doubles back into the middle pocket. The doubling of this particular red is easier to gauge than the last double because the line of the red to the cushion is going to be straighter for the red ball returning to indicated pocket. Strike cue ball at sufficient speed for position on black ball by striking cue ball at 8 o'clock when cue ball will follow desired path as shown.

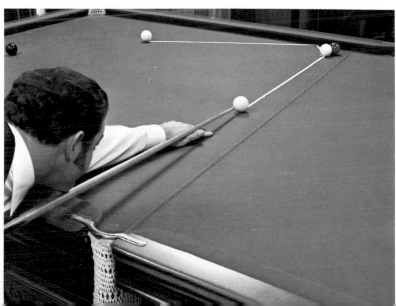

54B

The red ball is in a position for a Marker's double. By this I mean sending the red ball straight ahead to the side cushion, top cushion, side cushion and middle pocket. Position on the black ball is assured and if the red ball is missed, there is a strong possibility of reasonable safety being obtained. The cutting of the red ball into the corner pocket is a distinctly risky shot, as the ball may be left in the jaws if under, or over, cut. I prefer the Marker's double and use it quite often. It is not a difficult shot to play when I have gained a knowledge of angles of the table I am playing on. Striking point on cue ball is 15, stunning the cue ball to a stop on contact position shown for ideal position on the black ball.

Plant Shots

There are various types of plant shots that occur in snooker. Firstly there is the plant shot with balls touching that are not on to a pocket, but can be made on by pocketing the front ball, having struck the back ball on its correct contact point.

Secondly there is the plant shot where a back ball can be made 'in-off' the front ball. In making the far ball in the plant position shown in Plate 55A, the secret is the correct contact of the cue ball on to the right area of the nearest object ball. From the line of the two object balls to the jaw of the middle pocket it would appear that the front object ball would have to be struck on the right hand side (the obvious looking side). The contact point, however, is on the opposite side. Striking the nearest object ball on the left will squeeze that ball off to the right, and that near object ball will, in turn, carry the further object ball off to the right itself when the cue ball goes off to the left. With practice you can learn to contact on to the nearest red ball with the right contact (thin or thick depending on how much you intend to deflect the far object ball). In playing this shot, cue ball can be struck anywhere around its circumference, and at any speed.

55A – Plant Shots (Balls Touching – Front Ball)

Here you see me playing the shot three quarters full on to the left side of the first object ball deflecting the second object ball from off the plant line as indicated by the white mark on the cushion jaw to centre of pocket.

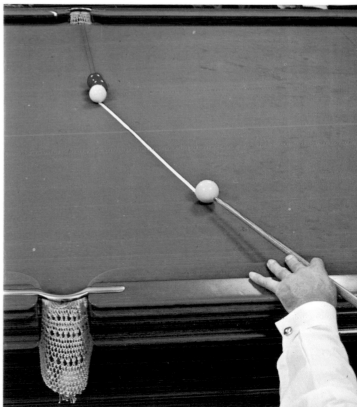

55A

55B – Plant Shots (Balls Apart – Front Ball)

A similar position to Plate 55A with the two balls planted on the same side of the jaw to the pocket opening; the difference this time is that the balls are apart. The far ball can again be made into the middle pocket but, because the balls are apart, on this occasion, the cue ball must be aimed to the right side of the nearest ball, so that the nearest ball goes off on line contacting the far ball on the correct point of contact, sending the far ball off on line to the pocket.

My technique for this particular shot is to sight the near object ball as a *cue* ball on to the far object ball in establishing the far object ball's line to the pocket. I then sight the area on the cushion in the background that the near object ball has to take, in striking the far object ball, to send it off on line to the pocket, and I simply get back behind the cue ball and aim the second object ball to the area I have picked out on the cushion. Be sure to play the shot with sufficient speed for the far object ball to reach the pocket.

Note the intended path of the cue ball on to the first object ball and the intended path of the first object ball on to the second object ball as marked in white. The contact point of the first object ball will send the second object ball along its intended path shown in red. The line of the first object ball on to the second object ball is taken to a point on the side cushion marked with a white mark. My sighting technique is to aim the first red ball from the angle to the cue ball in position shown to the white marker on the side cushion.

55B

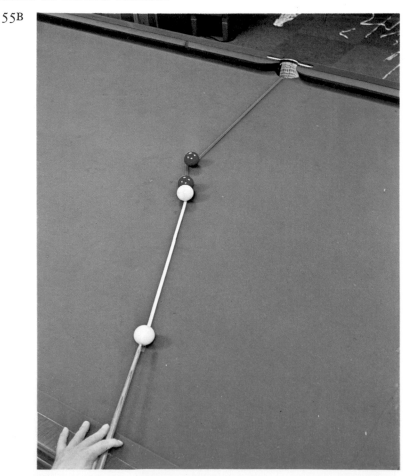

55C – **Plant Shots (Balls Touching – Back Ball)**

A situation where I have established that the line of the two object balls and the intended centre pocket are at right angles. I now realize that the back ball in this particular plant touching or to within 3 mm (⅛th inch) apart cannot be missed into the intended centre pocket. To send it off to the right, contact point is on the left – thick or thin. Again the shot can be made by striking the cue ball anywhere around its circumference, and at any speed. The shot cannot be missed as the back ball can only 'break-away' square.

55C

55D – Plant Shots (Balls Apart – Back Balls, Red and Black)

The picture shows a position of five reds adjacent to the black ball. You are looking at the shot from behind the cue ball as I see it. There does not appear to be a ball on, but this is one of the occasions when a big break can commence by seeing an angle where one red ball can be played 'in-off' another red ball to commence the break. From the position left me when I approached the table, I could see that red A could be played 'in-off' red B to the corner pocket. It was also obvious if I stunned the cue ball to a stop on red A, that red C would block my ideal position on the black for the same corner pocket. On closer examination, however, I could also see by stunning the cue ball to a dead stop on red A, that I could continue the break by making the black ball 'in-off' red ball D, thus opening the way for what could be a substantial break.

In the first of the two shots required in making red A and then the black ball as described, I aim red ball A half a ball on to red B to take intended path as shown to pocket. Striking point on cue ball – 15 with a softish stroke to give red A every chance of getting into the closed, corner pocket at that angle.

55E

55E – Plant Shots (Balls Apart – Back Balls, Red and Black)

Following on from Plate 55D, in taking the black ball, I use a similar technique of sending the black ball straight ahead for half ball contact on to the red ball for 'in-off' into the corner pocket. Striking point on cue ball in potting black is 14, and a firm stroke is required to send black firmly on to red ball and into corner pocket. Ideal position on to the red ball covering the path of the black ball to the pocket will be achieved.

Snookering

Laying snookers is a very important part of the game. Snookers can be played in the early part of a frame to get your opponent on the defensive and into trouble by forcing him to go off a cushion or around two or more cushions to hit the ball on (as there may still be 12 or 13 reds left at that stage). It is quite possible that your opponent will safely negotiate the snooker by hitting a red or reds that are on, which will give you the opportunity to commence what could be a frame winning break. Usually, however, snookers are employed later in a frame when a player needs the advantage of getting his opponent into trouble by laying a snooker with perhaps only one red left on the table, again looking for a leave should his opponent hit or even miss, the ball on. With the Foul Snooker and Play Again Rules that are now in the game of snooker, it is quite possible to get an advantage over your opponent with a snooker at that stage.

In the main, however, snookers are played for when there are not sufficient points left on the table towards the end of a frame for a player to win. The player now is forced to lay snookers in gaining the points allowed should his opponent fail to strike the ball on, from any such snooker laid. In attempting to lay snookers try to find an angle that you can play so that, besides your opponent being snookered on the ball on, distance between ball on and the cue ball has to be considered as well, adding to your opponent's worries and testing his knowledge of angles to the full.

56A – Snookering (Colours on Spot, One Red, Baulk End)

The last red ball is towards the bottom end of the table. I require a snooker to win. My intention here is to play thin to the outside edge of the red, cutting the red on to the first side cushion, and across to the opposite side cushion, and in behind the baulk colours along intended path shown. Cue ball to travel to bottom cushion on to side cushion and back down to finish with the black or the pink covering the red and putting distance between the cue ball and object ball. There is a possibility that other balls may finish between cue ball and the red ball as well. Striking point on the cue ball for this shot is 10 o'clock. Correct strength of stroke is extremely important here so that red ball travels the two intended cushions and back near the centre of the table, away from either corner pocket, with the cue ball at the top of the table, above the black ball.

56B – Snookering (Colours on Spot – One Red, Spot End)

The last red is at the opposite, top, end of the table with cue ball in position as shown. Requiring a snooker from this position I have the same thoughts again of not only acquiring a snooker but putting distance between cue ball and object ball, thus making the shot doubly difficult for my opponent. The way I would play this particular shot would be to aim full at the red ball striking the cue ball at 15 with sufficient strength to drive the object ball around two cushions along intended path shown, checking the cue ball in behind the black ball.

From this position I seldom play the cue ball from the red ball to the side cushion in behind the black ball, at the same time driving the red ball on to the top cushion back down the table, as at this angle it is very easy to misjudge the shot and have the cue ball return off the side cushion, meeting up and making contact with the red returning from the top cushion. Nine times out of ten, when this happens, the red ball is left on.

56B

88

56C – Snookering (Blue, Pink, Black)

A situation of blue, pink and black balls being left and a snooker required. A safe shot to try here, requiring a snooker to win, is to play thin to the left edge of the blue ball, cutting the blue over to the centre of the baulk cushion at sufficient speed for the cue ball to travel to baulk cushion, then side cushion, in an endeavour to get behind the black or pink balls. It is the type of shot I often look for as, in failing to gain the pink, I at least have acquired a reasonable safety shot. Striking point on the cue ball in sending the blue ball along the desired path, and the cue ball around its intended journey, is dead centre, 14.

56C

Out of Snookers

Being forced to play out of snookers successfully, requires a similar knowledge to laying snookers and playing safety shots, i.e. a good knowledge of natural angles on a billiard table. There are very few snookers that could not be played out of, with a good knowledge of those angles.

It is not always getting out of the snooker that can be the problem, particularly with the class of player that I am continually opposed to, but hitting the object ball and getting it safe after successfully negotiating the snooker.

With these thoughts in mind, I may consider playing around angles with a dead strength shot, that would leave the cue ball as close to the object ball as possible so that after I have hit the ball on, or perhaps unluckily missed it, my opponent will have no chance of pocketing that ball.

Then again I may purposely play to get out of the shot by power, driving the object ball as far away from the cue ball as is possible after negotiating the snooker. My intention here would be to have as much distance between the balls as possible making it difficult for my opponent to score from the position left him. Whichever way I decide to play the shot, I will look for a way that is as foolproof as possible by using one cushion where I can in preference to two, or two cushions where I can in preference to three, and so on. I often employ the swerve shot to swing around the offending ball in getting out of a snooker, or apply the quicker turn by using a massé shot. It depends *so much* on the state of the game, and the number of points left on the table when I am confronted with these situations.

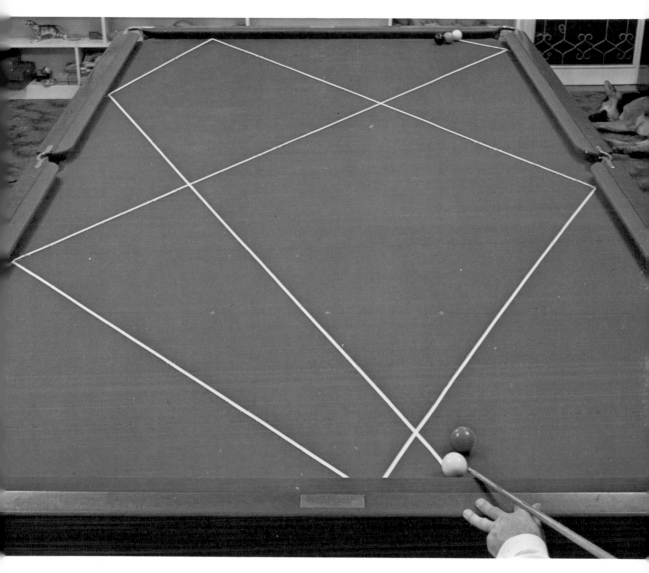

57A

Plate 57A shows a shot I recently had to play when snookered on the blue in behind the pink, as shown, with the black covering one side of the blue as well. I successfully negotiated the snooker off seven cushions as shown, and was quite confident of doing so before I played the shot, because of my knowledge of angles in the first instance, and the beautiful Heiron & Smith table I was playing on, in the second instance. Striking point on the cue ball for this shot 4 o'clock, with a very powerful stroke required to travel the seven cushions.

57B – Out of Snookers

Another way of getting out of a seemingly impossible snooker. There are usually several ways of getting out of snookers because of the various angles that can be taken on a billiard table. The shot that I preferred to play in this instance recently was to play on to the jaw of the top cushion, deflecting back on to the opposite jaw of the side cushion, cue ball finally travelling along the face of the top cushion as shown, to make contact with the blue ball. Striking point on the cue ball for this shot, 15. A firm stroke required so that backspin applied to the cue ball will remain on the cue ball on its journey to the first cushion, thus assisting the cue ball to stay down on the table, and not jump in the jaws, as so often can happen on billiard tables.

57C – **Out of Snookers**

An extremely nasty situation, where a medium-paced shot with strong left hand side resulted in my cue ball, travelling the indicated path to top cushion, returning to the bottom cushion, and on to the blue ball. Striking point on the cue ball, 10 o'clock. Correct speed of stroke for this particular shot is of paramount importance so that the cue ball will have the intended amount of spin applied to it when it hits the first cushion (top cushion).

Safety Play

Safety play I consider is a very technical, but important part of snooker play, particularly as played by professionals in the top bracket of snooker. The standard of snooker today among the top flight professionals, particularly in matches between Ray Reardon and myself, is that frame after frame can be won or lost depending on who gets the first red ball. The first player on so many occasions, will win the frame.

In striving to get in first, strong safety play can be a great ally. It can be the means of getting in first, for slowing your opponent down if the match is slipping away from you, and can be a strong tactical move halfway through a frame, or at the very end of a frame.

I look at successful snooker in three ways. Good, long, consistent potting, strong, reliable and consistent break building, and strong, determined safety play. I have won ever so many frames over my years as a professional player, through strong safety play in the first instance, the creation of the slightest opening when a good pot has got me in and the further result of a good break that has clinched the frame. They are tactics that have worked for me and helped one of my main ambitions to be the outstanding tournament winner in the game. Today I hold that distinction, having won more tournaments than any other living snooker player.

I will continue with the same techniques until such time as my game in one department or another tends to slip, when I will be forced to look for other techniques in my determination to stay near the top of the game.

Safety play can be a knowledge of angles, with keen eyesight for hitting thin edges at long distance, with cueing ability to play shots at the right strength. My technique at safety play is to keep as much distance between object ball and cue ball as possible, to leave my opponent with the cue ball as close to a cushion as I can possibly leave it, and, most importantly, to leave the object ball in an area where the pocketing of that object ball will be extremely difficult.

58A – Safety Play (Black Only – Thin Edge – Black to Win)

If confronted with the situation shown, I will play a thin edge on the black, cutting it to the middle of the top cushion and bringing the cue ball around the angle along the intended path shown for what I consider would be a good safety shot.

In this case I will play a thin edge on the black ball because the cue ball is travelling from the baulk end to the top end with the nap and will not have its path to the black ball influenced by nap restriction, as it would have if going against the nap. The danger aspect of playing to the thin edges of balls any distance away when playing into the nap is that, should the cue ball turn off its course by only a slight degree, it could completely miss the edge of the black ball, and cost you the frame. Striking point above centre at 13.

58B –Safety Play
(Black Only –Thick Contact –Black to Win)

The opposite situation, with the object ball at the bottom end of the table, and the cue ball at the top end of the table. A nasty position at any time. Now I am forced to play into the nap. There is *no way*, on any table, that I will attempt a thin edge contact on to the black ball.

You cannot play half ball shots from this position as both balls will travel approximately the same distance, and you are most likely to bring the black ball around for an easy potting position for your opponent. In most cases when I am forced to play into the nap over the length of the table and cannot pot the black ball, I will look for a shot that can be played using the thick contact on to the black to bring the black ball to my end of the table and leave my cue ball at the opposite end, thereby forcing my opponent to play his next shot with as much distance between the balls as I can manage. I concentrate on getting the black ball as safe as I can to the end cushion, in preference to concentrating on getting the cue ball safe.

By striking the cue ball in this case at 12 o'clock, I will play into the black three-quarters full on the left hand side, doubling the black ball straight down the table at sufficient speed as to leave it as close to the centre of the top cushion (as per path shown) and the cue ball on to the side cushion, along its intended path.

58B

59 – Swerve Shot

In playing to swerve the cue ball, raise your cue butt as shown and strike the cue ball on the side of intended swerve. The cue ball struck on the right side curves to the right as it approaches the object ball. The curve of the cue ball is controlled by the striking point on the cue ball, the angle of the cue down on to the cue ball and the power of the shot.

In attempting a swerve shot, your aim at the cue ball is governed by the anticipated curve. When attempting to curve around the blue from position shown to hit the red at the opposite end of the table, I intend to swerve left. My aim is approximately 8 cm (3″) out to the right of the blue ball and, when I strike the cue ball low and left at 7 o'clock at a comfortable speed to reach the red, the cue ball will take the intended arc. In attempting to swerve around the blue ball on the opposite side of the table, the same technique is used but the striking point on the cue ball becomes 5 o'clock. With practice you learn to play this shot at exactly the right speed.

60 – Massé Shot

A sharp massé. In setting up to play this shot your stance is upright. Stand as close to and face the table as much as possible. Turn the back of your bridge hand towards the shot. My bridge hand grip is taken on two fingers only and there is a lot of pressure being applied on those fingers to steady my bridge hand for this all important shot.

With my cueing hand, my cue hand grip is taken with the thumb, and first three fingers. My little finger is under the cue butt. Cueing arm is bent as shown and a short grip on cue is a must. Having chalked your tip carefully in attempting one of the most difficult shots in the game and with the cue slanting back against your cheek, play down on the cue ball to massé to the left at 11 o'clock. Do not play through the ball into the cloth as you will only succeed in pushing the cue ball out without getting it back.

A massé is a touch shot where the cue tip must come down briskly to nip down on to the cue ball at 11 o'clock, and up again. Do not play through the ball at all. The cue striking the cue ball at 11 o'clock after having aimed the cue ball safely to the right of the offending object ball or balls will push a little further out to the right of your intended aim in the first instance. The 'push off' of the cue ball from the cue tip becomes spent, and the left hand spin applied viciously by the cue tip nipping on to and off the cue ball, will twist the cue ball to the object ball.

It is extremely important on massé shots to nip the cue ball (11 o'clock) with the right speed. This is a shot which must be practised to bend the path of the cue ball out and back as quickly as intended. To massé the ball the other way, the shot is played the same, however the cue ball is struck on the opposite side (1 o'clock).

Note the bridge hand position for this shot.

Trick Shots

PART 2

Contents (List of Trick Shots)

Introduction to Trick Shots

Whenever I give exhibitions, and that is very often indeed in these days when snooker, billiards and pool are among the most popular games to play and watch, I always finish with a selection of trick shots.

Occasionally, perhaps when some exhibition matches have been too one-sided, an audience may lack the customary tension and excitement that one can feel during matches. But the concluding trick shot exhibition never fails to win them over and send them home happy with an evening's entertainment.

My trick shots can be kind to me, too. I may have fluffed some shots in matchplay, but after I have brought off some amazing trick shots (and amazing is the word for some of the shots in this book), they would refuse to believe I am not the greatest player ever to have picked up a cue!

That is one of the secrets of trick shot making. You can perfect them and get them right every time (well, almost!) even when you are mucking up simple, straight pots. But it is no easy thing. You will have to practise some of them for many hours before you can be confident that you will get it right.

The main point I am making, however, is that slick, spectacular trick shots can be brought off by average players who are prepared to practise them. And what a glow of satisfaction you will get when you set up an 'impossible' shot before your family and friends, and then send the balls unerringly to their destination.

I like playing trick shots, and always enjoy the feeling of having brought off a good shot and amazed an audience.

This section shows trick shots of varying degrees of difficulty, with explicit instructions and a colour photographic guide of how to play them. Some will take the average player a fair while to perfect and there are others where I am, perhaps, showing off and which may be beyond the range of the average player. But do try them all — they are all achievable and the pictures of moving balls and balls in the air attest that there are no set ups here. I would never offer a shot that I could not play myself, but I would not guarantee to get some of the harder ones, such as the Flying White Horse, or the Kangaroo Hop, first time.

There are other shots that I guarantee you will master very quickly, and one or two that you cannot fail to get first and every time provided that you can hit a ball reasonably straight. One such shot is a sneaky push shot where you will clear the obstructing balls with a cannon and keep your cue going to pocket a red. In another, pocketing the ball when planted, you cannot fail to pocket the planted ball if you make contact with the cue ball anywhere but dead centre around the circumference of the red.

Shots like that are in the book because, like all trick shots, they are fun to play and they will give the beginner a glow of success that will lead him to work on some of the harder shots.

Perhaps the best thing about trick shot making is the hours of enjoyment they will give you when you are playing alone. You cannot always get Fred from next door to come and have a game with you, and you may get sick of straight practice, although you shouldn't and Part I has an immensely varied practice schedule that should make practice a challenge. However, I am sure you will never get sick of setting up and making trick shots. My only regret is that, with my straight practice and playing schedule, I don't get enough time to keep all my trick shots up to date. I have seen many hundreds of trick shots, more than I can remember, but I have a working range of over 300 trick and fancy shots that I draw on for play in front of the audience.

Of course I don't succeed with all of them all of the time. I suppose I have about a 95% success rate, but it is part of the fun for the onlookers to see a shot come unstuck. These shots have to be played with a spirit of good humour and a bit of clowning. After the serious business of matchplay, it is nice to have a bit of laughter and give-and-take with the audience.

There are a few shots here that are deliberate deception shots, such as the one when I 'kiss' the blue into the centre pocket. A groan goes up at such a badly missed shot, but I retrieve the situation with my nicely-timed kiss.

Some of the shots in this section I have borrowed from players I have seen presenting them in many parts of the world, some are my own and others I have seen played in Australian clubs or have had suggested to me by club players. There is one shot that was made as a fluke by a raw novice, but was so spectacular that I had to use it again.

Bear in mind that most often trick shots presented can be played on less than full size tables. The angles are the same, although speed of stroke to control distance will have to be adjusted. By quick experimentation you will be able to allow for the difference in table size. Also the shots include snooker, pool, and billiards situations. No one has been left out!

Good trick shot making comes from confidence. If you don't expect to make the shot, it's certain that you won't. Confidence comes from practice and the sure feeling that you should have about the cueing and strength of stroke for a particular shot.

In summary, the three elements for successful trick shot making are:

★Correct setting up of the proposed shot.

★Correct striking of the cue tip onto the cue ball.

★To have the right strength of stroke so that the right speed is achieved.

I have covered all these aspects in my explanations of the shots presented in this book. I have worked to give a complete and yet easily readable summary of the shot and how it is played and feel sure that I have revealed the inner workings of these mysterious and impossible shots.

I look forward to hearing that you have enjoyed them.

I — Blue Ball — Centre Pocket

DESCRIPTION: The idea of my first trick shot is to move the blue ball out of the cluster of reds on the side cushion into the centre pocket. It is an impossible looking shot, but it is quite an easy trick shot.

TO SET UP: Make sure the 3 reds and blue are all touching one another and all 4 touching cushion.

Front red 6 mm (¼″) away from red immediately in front of blue and half a ball out from cushion.

HOW TO PLAY: Strike cue ball at 6 o'clock with a medium strength stroke to force blue along cushion and in off red over centre pocket. The draw action on cue ball will force blue ball to go ahead and into pocket.

MAIN POINTS: Strike cue ball at 6 o'clock.

2 – Yellow Ball – Corner Pocket

DESCRIPTION: In this impossible looking shot the yellow ball is to be pocketed into the top corner pocket, as indicated by the yellow line.

TO SET UP: All 7 reds and yellow ball are hard on top cushion and touching.

Cue ball and first object red are positioned as shown.

Second object red (lone red near end cushion) is 13 mm (½") off face of cushion, 40 cm (16") from yellow ball.

HOW TO PLAY: Contact point of cue ball on to first red is half ball, driving red ball to side cushion and back to end red as indicated by red line.

Cue ball will leave the first red, making a cannon on to the lone red that is blocking the path of the yellow ball to corner pocket as indicated by white line, doubling red ball on to end cushion and out along short red line.

Cue ball will follow path on to top cushion as indicated by short white line, thus clearing path for yellow ball.

MAIN POINTS: This is a medium strength stroke. Striking point on cue ball is 15.

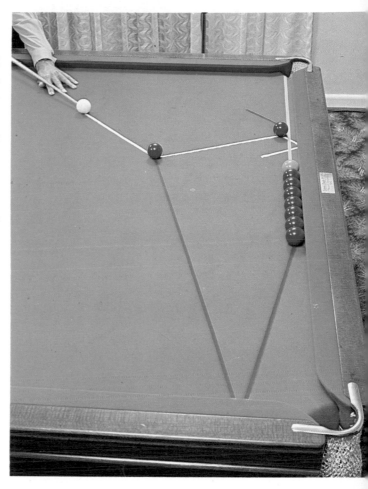

3 — The Zigzag Shot

DESCRIPTION: And now to pocket the yellow after making contact with all 11 red balls. This is an exceptionally clever trick shot, driving all 11 reds across the table to finally pocket yellow with cue ball. It is a spectacular shot, but an easy one to master.

TO SET UP: Place balls as shown in photo. Place cue ball near green spot.

HOW TO PLAY: Strike cushion first as indicated by white marker so cue ball returns off cushion on to first red, cannons back on to cushion and out on to second red, and so on until it finally reaches yellow ball.

SECOND PICTURE: Note red balls fanning out across table as cue ball moves down to meet up with yellow ball.

MAIN POINTS: This is a power shot and cue ball must be struck at 4 o'clock. Strike cushion (white marker) correctly as correct contact must take place on first red. This shot should be persevered with to find correct point of contact on side cushion.

4 — The Snake Shot

DESCRIPTION: One of the easier trick shots, but it gives a very satisfying effect. You should use it early in your repertoire to create the right impression of mastery with your audience and hope it will soften the blow if a later shot goes wrong.

TO SET UP: Space red balls 8 cm (3″) apart and form, as nearly as possible, the shape illustrated.

HOW TO PLAY: To pocket blue ball off the end of the snake string of red balls, aim cue ball full at first red ball, striking cue ball dead centre at 14 with a distinct power shot.

A chain reaction takes place on the red balls to make the blue ball into the corner pocket.

SECOND PICTURE: Note how red balls have fanned out following chain reaction as second last red is about to contact the last red, thus sending blue on its intended journey.

MAIN POINTS: Make sure the reds are properly spaced so that at no time does any one red ball fail to make thick enough contact on to the next red to ensure that the chain reaction will take place through to the blue.

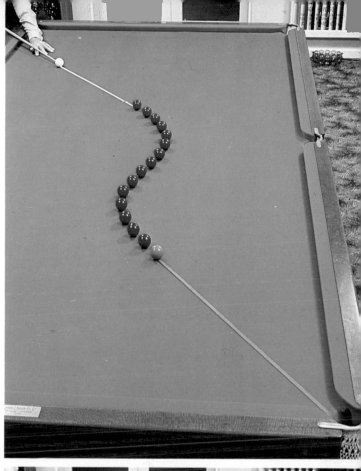

5 — The Blue Mystery

DESCRIPTION: A spectacular shot which makes the blue ball, away from the cluster of 2 reds as shown, into the pocket.

TO SET UP: Place 2 reds touching in cluster just off centre line of table, as shown.

Aim reds to left side of pocket on left of blue line looking back from camera.

Place blue in centre and touching both reds, thus forming the cluster.

The 3 pairs of planted red balls are to be placed evenly 20 cm (8″) apart.

The 3 balls in each plant, on left looking back from camera, are to be on a straight line from second red to left side of pocket and blue line.

All 3 pairs of planted balls are touching, each of 3 balls on right looking back from camera are at a slight angle, as shown by red lines going out of picture on right side looking back from camera.

HOW TO PLAY: Contact of cue ball on to first red ball, as shown by white line, is half ball contact.

Cue ball is to be struck at 14, cannoning off red onto blue, cue ball continuing away from blue on white line shown.

Second red shown in cluster will follow red line shown, making contact on to first pair of planted balls.

First ball in cluster will move out on red line shown, sending left side ball in first cluster on to left side ball in second cluster, and so on to left side ball in third cluster.

Other red lines indicate how three pairs of red balls have split apart allowing blue ball to follow the blue line.

SECOND PICTURE: Note how the first two sets of planted red balls have already spread apart, with the red from left of second cluster moving ahead to split the final pair of planted balls, thus clearing the path of blue ball heading to pocket.

MAIN POINTS: Contact of cue ball on to first red is half ball on left side. Striking point on cue ball must be 14.

6 — Ring around the White

DESCRIPTION: How can I pocket the blue ball from a seemingly impossible snooker, with a ring of red balls around the cue ball?

HOW TO PLAY: The idea of this shot is to play the cue ball on to the side cushion at speed so that cue ball rebounds off the cushion, through the air, to make contact on to the blue. This shot is to be played with medium strength.

It is very important to strike the cue ball at 12 o'clock with a downward stroke, by having your cue butt raised as shown in photograph one.

If you are not clearing the ring of reds, apply more power. If cue ball is jumping off the table, too much power is being applied.

As in all trick shots, correct striking of cue tip on to the cue ball and playing with the right strength is vital for success.

MAIN POINTS: Strike cue ball high, preferably at 12 o'clock. Raise your cue butt and play down on cue ball forcing it to jump so that it is already in the air when it reaches the side cushion. Rebounding off side cushion will force cue ball higher in the air, up over reds as shown in the second photo and bouncing across table to meet the blue.

7 — Kangaroo Hop

DESCRIPTION: The idea here is to leap over the intervening reds to pocket the pink. It is a great trick shot requiring a high degree of control as you must not only jump the reds but keep the ball on course. This type of shot must not be played in straight snooker as jumping balls over intervening balls are foul shots.

TO SET UP: Place balls as shown, with the white close enough to the cushion to allow a high bridge that will assist a downward stroke.

HOW TO PLAY: To get the cue ball to jump, you must strike it at 12 o'clock with a downward stroke by raising your cue butt as shown. It is a very powerful shot. Notice the height of cue butt which shows the angle of the downward stroke that is essential to get the cue ball to hurdle over the two reds.

SECOND PICTURE: In the second picture my expression indicates the power used in getting the cue ball up over the reds and heading towards the pink ball in the diagonal corner pocket.

MAIN POINTS: Strike cue ball at 12 o'clock. A power shot will ensure cue ball rising over intervening red balls.

8 – Ring around the Rosey

DESCRIPTION: To pocket the blue ball into the corner pocket from this difficult position I will have to send it cannoning off a half circle of 11 reds. This is a beautiful and delicate shot that will bring a gasp of appreciation from your audience, even if it is only your wife, children and the dog.

TO SET UP: Make a ring of reds around blue as shown. Distance between the reds is about 2.5 cm (1″).

HOW TO PLAY: In making the blue ball into the corner pocket, the idea is to play the cue ball full into the blue ball, sending that ball on to the side cushion, from where it will return around the ring of reds into the corner pocket.

Use a medium strength stroke for this shot. Striking point on the cue ball is 15, with the cue butt slightly raised to get over the ring of reds.

SECOND PICTURE: The second picture shows the cue ball stunned to an im-

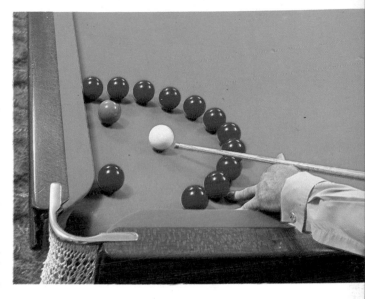

mediate halt by cue tip having struck at 15. The blue ball has fanned out reds on its way to the pocket.

MAIN POINTS: Strike cue ball at 15 so that no jump effect will take place, as cue butt had to be raised to get over ring of reds. Play medium strength stroke for blue to reach corner pocket.

9 — The Obstacle Shot

DESCRIPTION: Pocketing the blue from out of a snooker, with one or two obstacles in the way!

TO SET UP: Set up white and blue balls as shown, and having predetermined the path of the balls place obstacles (non-breakable for beginners) around the table.

HOW TO PLAY: Having recently found myself confronted with this situation when I was on the blue (with one or two obstacles in the way!), I decided the only way out was to use five cushions, striking the cue ball from off the green spot with a lot of power at 3 o'clock. The cue ball followed the path as indicated by the white lines to successfully pocket the blue ball.

SECOND PICTURE: Note the obstacles confronting me on this shot.

MAIN POINTS: Strike first cushion, as shown, with medium to hard strength. Strike cue ball at 3 o'clock. Place obstacles as close as you dare to the pre-planned path of the cue ball.

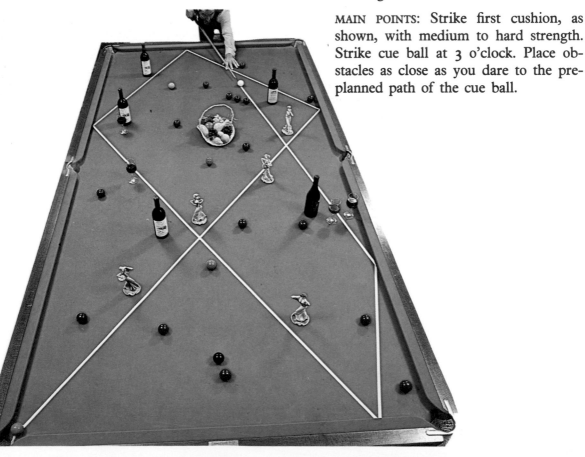

10 — Swerve Shot

DESCRIPTION: To swerve around intervening ball to contact the object ball.

HOW TO PLAY: In playing to swerve the cue ball, raise your cue butt as shown and strike the cue ball on the side of intended swerve. The cue ball struck on the right side curves to the right as it approaches the object ball. The curve of the cue ball is controlled by the striking point on the cue ball, the angle of the cue down on to the cue ball and the power of the shot.

In attempting a swerve shot, your aim at the cue ball is governed by the anticipated curve. When attempting to curve around the blue from position shown to hit the red at the opposite end of the table, I intend to swerve left. My aim is approximately 8 cm (3″) out to the right of the blue ball and, when I strike the cue ball low and left at 7 o'clock at a comfortable speed to reach the red, the cue ball will take the intended arc. In attempting to swerve around the blue ball on the opposite side of the table, the same technique is used but the striking point on the cue ball becomes 5 o'clock. With practice you learn to play this shot at exactly the right speed.

MAIN POINTS: Not a trick shot, but a very exciting shot to watch and to succeed with. A very handy shot for straight snooker.

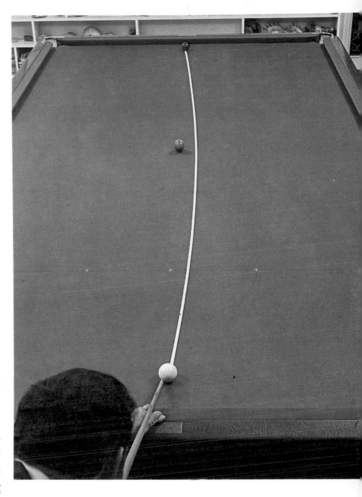

11 — A Massé Shot

DESCRIPTION: To swing in an arc around intervening balls, as shown.

HOW TO PLAY: A sharp massé. In setting up to play this shot your stance is upright. Stand as close to the table and face it as much as possible. Turn the back of your bridge hand towards the shot. My bridge hand grip is taken on two fingers only and there is a lot of pressure being applied on those fingers to steady my bridge hand for this all important shot.

Cue hand grip is taken with the thumb, and first three fingers, with the

little finger under the cue butt. The cueing arm is bent as shown, and a short grip on cue is a must. Having chalked your tip carefully in attempting one of the most difficult shots in the game and with the cue slanting back against your cheek, play down on the cue ball to massé to the left at 11 o'clock. Do not play through the ball into the cloth as you will only push the cue ball out without getting it back.

A massé is a touch shot where the cue tip must come down quickly to nip down on to the cue ball at 11 o'clock, and up again. Do not play through the ball at all. The cue striking the cue ball at 11 o'clock after having aimed the cue ball safely to the right of the offending object ball or balls will push a little further out to the right of your intended aim in the first instance. The 'push off' of the cue ball from the cue tip becomes spent, and the left hand spin applied viciously by the cue tip nipping on to and off the cue ball, will twist the cue ball to the object ball.

It is extremely important on massé shots to nip the cue ball (11 o'clock) with the right speed. This is a shot which must be practised so that the cue ball will bend out and back as quickly as intended. To massé the ball the other way, the shot is the same, but the cue ball is struck on the opposite side (1 o'clock).

Note the bridge hand position for this shot.

MAIN POINTS: Always a neat and attractive shot. I am asked more questions about this shot than any other. With practice, and by carrying out my instructions carefully, you will succeed with the massé.

12 — Push Shot

DESCRIPTION: Here's a shot that often crops up at snooker. It is quite easily played if one employs a little trick to make the 'speed of the hand deceive the eye'. Most players confronted with a shot like this would consider that the back red is not on for the centre pocket because of the covering front red near the cue ball. However the back ball is quite an easy ball to pocket, and this is the way to go about it.

HOW TO PLAY: Aim your cue tip to dead centre on cue ball playing straight into first red at half ball contact. Play a push shot as shown with the cue passing through the white and first red. That will clear the path for the cue to follow on and strike the second red direct into the centre pocket.

PICTURES: Picture one shows shot at address.

Picture two shows cue ball and first red ball clearing the way — cue having gone through to strike intended red, sending it off on line for pocket.

MAIN POINTS: Strike cue ball dead centre with as hard a stroke as possible. Make sure the cue drives through on a level plane so that good contact will be made of cue tip on to second red. The shot must be played at speed so that cue is not seen as having gone right through to second red. A sneaky shot!

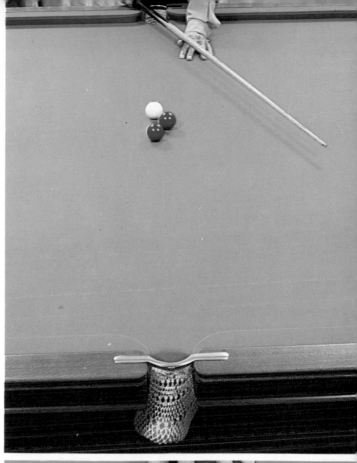

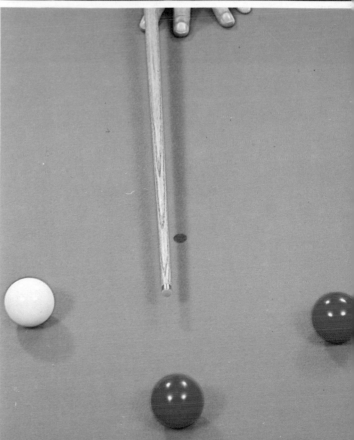

13 — Four Reds in the One Shot

DESCRIPTION: Here I am setting out to pocket all four red balls into four different pockets in the one stroke.

TO SET UP: Yellow and blue are touching, planting yellow ball to white marker on side cushion just above red ball.

Place red on other side of blue in a straight plant to centre of pocket.

Cue ball back on position shown, 20 cm (8") from blue ball.

HOW TO PLAY: Play full into blue with a medium strength stroke, striking cue ball at 6 o'clock. Red against blue plays into centre pocket.

Yellow will cross table on path indicated by yellow line to pocket second red.

Meanwhile blue ball travels path of blue line to pocket third red ball.

Finally white ball draws back right down side cushion on path shown by white line to pocket fourth and final red ball.

MAIN POINTS: Three balls in cluster (red, blue, yellow) must be placed as described. All 3 balls must be touching. Remember to strike cue ball with a very firm stroke at 6 o'clock.

14 — Putting the Balls to Sleep

DESCRIPTION: A pretty shot which pockets all three balls in the one shot.

TO SET UP: Place yellow ball on pink spot.

Position red, planting yellow ball directly at white marker indicated on side cushion immediately below top left corner pocket.

Cue ball on baulk line, 5 cm (2″) into hand from yellow spot.

HOW TO PLAY: Aim at red half a ball on left side with a medium strength stroke, striking cue ball just above centre at 13.

Yellow ball will plant off along yellow line shown to centre of pocket.

Red ball will follow red line shown to centre of right top corner pocket.

Cue ball will continue on after contact on to red along extended white line shown, also to top left corner pocket but ahead of yellow.

MAIN POINTS: Place yellow exactly on pink spot. Place red touching against yellow aiming to side of corner pocket. Contact point on to red half ball. Strike cue ball dead centre with a medium strength stroke.

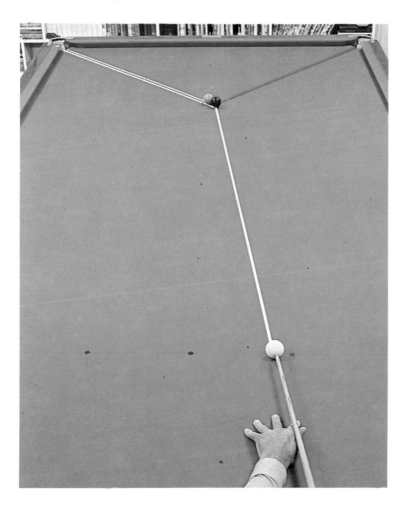

15 — Pocketing the Ball (when planted)

DESCRIPTION: Here is one unmissable trick shot, in a situation where the line between two touching object balls and a pocket are at right angles.

TO SET UP: To pocket red ball into either centre pocket from position shown, place red on blue spot.

Plant yellow against and touching red ball straight down the line of spots as indicated by yellow line.

Place cue ball on brown spot.

HOW TO PLAY: Red ball can be played into either centre pocket as indicated by red lines. Contact cue ball on either side of red ball, thick or thin. Contact must be made on opposite side of red to intended pocket.

For example, to make red ball into left centre pocket, contact on to red a quarter thick or half thick on right side, thus sending red ball along left red line to left centre pocket.

Cue ball can be struck anywhere around its circumference but I recommend dead centre.

MAIN POINTS: In various positions if the line of the touching balls and the line of the back ball (or ball closest to cue ball) and a pocket are at right angles (keeping in mind the back ball can only break away at right angles because both balls are the same weight), the pocketing of that back ball cannot be missed. The player can inadvertently strike the cue ball anywhere around its circumference at any speed, catching that object ball thick or thin.

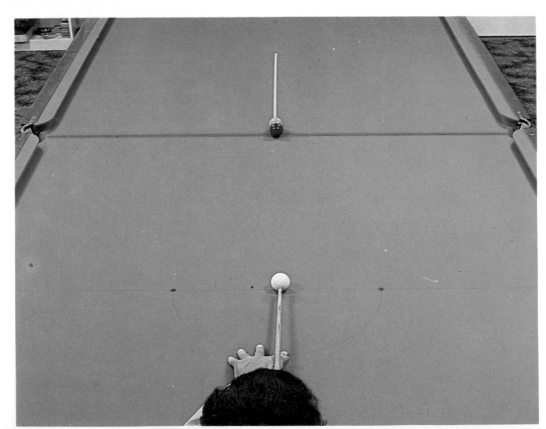

16 — Stymie Shot

DESCRIPTION: Pocketing the yellow ball from a cluster of red balls that would seem to bar the path to the pocket.

TO SET UP: All four balls in cluster are touching on line to centre pocket.

Yellow and closest red to camera are on line to centre pocket.

HOW TO PLAY: Aim cue ball for half ball contact on left of first red as shown by white line. Strike cue ball firmly above centre at 13, making cannon off first red on to yellow ball.

Reds will clear path to centre pocket for yellow ball to travel yellow line as shown.

MAIN POINTS: A smooth cue delivery is paramount here. Strike cue ball at 13, allowing cue to travel through, imparting top spin to white, which in turn will push yellow through to pocket.

17 — A Push Shot

DESCRIPTION: The object of this shot is to make the yellow from between the reds to the corner pocket.

TO SET UP: To make the yellow ball into the corner pocket as indicated by yellow line, all three object balls are touching hard against the bottom cushion. Place cue ball as shown, touching first red.

HOW TO PLAY: Address cue ball high with cue tip at 11 o'clock.

A medium strength push shot is the main essential required here.

Do not draw cue back and stroke the ball.

Place cue tip up to cue ball at 11 o'clock and push straight through.

Yellow ball will travel intended yellow line to pocket and the two red balls will stay out, having followed path indicated by red lines.

MAIN POINTS: All three object balls and cue ball must be touching. Place cue tip hard against cue ball at 11 o'clock. Push straight through with a soft to medium paced strength. Do not draw back. Do not stroke the ball.

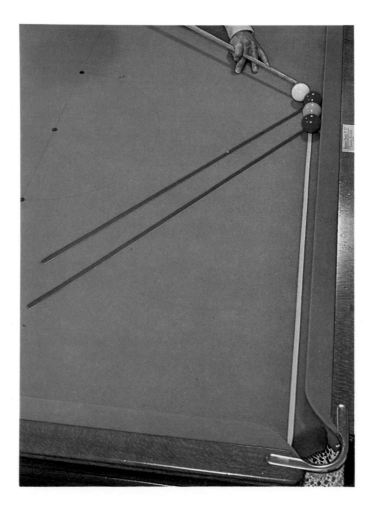

18 — Around the Table Cannon

DESCRIPTION: A long way for two points, but this brilliant looking shot can keep you in the game. An around the table cannon to meet the red ball above the centre pocket to make the cannon.

TO SET UP: Opponent's white is on the baulk line touching side cushion, red ball is touching opponent's white and cushion.

HOW TO PLAY: Aim one-third full on right side of opponent's white ball striking cue ball at 10 o'clock.

Play the stroke with sufficient strength to allow cue ball to travel path shown by white line to meet up with red ball travelling path shown by red line.

At the same time, correct timing will have the balls meeting as indicated above the centre pocket.

Opponent's white ball will travel directly across the baulk line out of the way.

MAIN POINTS: Contact opponent's white ball one-third on the right as described. Strike cue ball at 2 o'clock. Practice will make timing perfect, as is required for this shot.

19 — Kiss Cannon

DESCRIPTION: A pretty cannon and only one of the many kiss cannons that can be played.

TO SET UP: Place red hard up on bottom cushion 25 cm (10″) out from corner pocket. Cue ball straight out from red 25 cm (10″).

Opponent's white ball on top cushion 25 cm (10″) in from corner pocket.

HOW TO PLAY: From position shown, play seven-eighths full into red ball striking cue ball bottom dead centre at 6 o'clock.

Cue ball will rebound off red ball placed hard against bottom cushion 25cm (10″) from corner pocket, to follow white line shown to meet up with opponent's white ball at top end of table.

MAIN POINTS: Play seven-eights full on to left side of red ball striking cue ball at 6 o'clock. Cue ball will double kiss and rebound from red to intended opponent's white as shown.

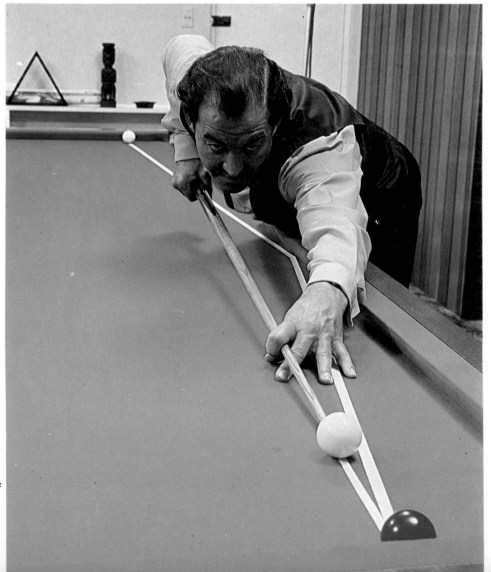

20 — Seven Cushion Cannon

DESCRIPTION: This is a really exciting shot, and one of the very few ways that a seven cushion cannon can be made on a billiard table.

TO SET UP: Place two object balls into position shown 15 cm (6″) out from top cushion. Cue ball on green spot.

HOW TO PLAY: Aim cue ball at white marker on side cushion, striking cue ball at 3 o'clock with a very firm stroke.

Cue ball to follow intended path of white line around seven cushions to complete the cannon.

This is not a natural angle shot as it has sidespin which takes the ball away from the natural path, but is one of the very few ways that a seven cushion cannon can be made.

MAIN POINTS: Strike cue ball at 3 o'clock and practise this shot until the right contact point is found off the first cushion and the right speed of stroke is achieved.

21 — Kiss around Angles

DESCRIPTION: Another kiss cannon around the angles.

TO SET UP: This time the red ball is hard up on bottom cushion under the nameplate, and the cue ball and object balls in positions shown.

HOW TO PLAY: Aim at red ball half a ball on right side, striking the cue ball at 6 o'clock with power.

Cue ball will rebound after receiving a double kiss off red, to follow white line as shown to make contact with four cushions before meeting up with opponent's white ball.

MAIN POINTS: Correct contact on the red ball, striking cue ball at 6 o'clock and with sufficient strength of stroke for the cue ball to travel journey indicated are the main essentials.

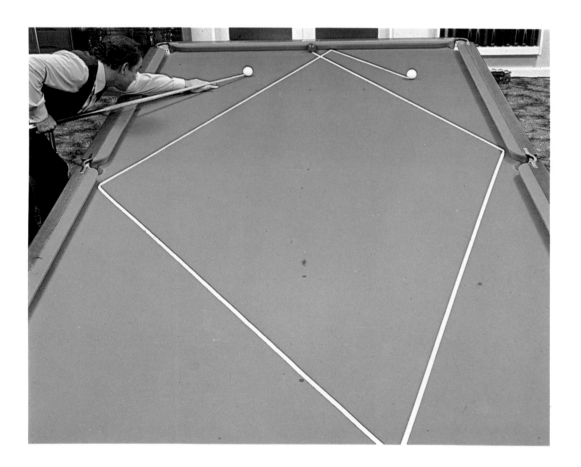

22 – Around the Table – Five Shot

DESCRIPTION: Around the table 5 shot when both balls are in baulk.

TO SET UP: Red ball in centre of bottom cushion 8 cm (3″) out.

Opponent's white ball 8 cm (3″) out from bottom cushion and 2.5 cm (1″) out from side cushion.

Place cue ball on green spot.

HOW TO PLAY: Aim at white marker indicated on side cushion.

Strike cue ball at 3 o'clock with power so that cue ball will travel intended white line as shown.

Cue ball will come in on to cushion at back of red, catching red approximately three-quarters full on left side, before travelling on as shown to contact opponent's white ball for 2, playing into the pocket for 3 to complete the 5 shot.

MAIN POINTS: Correct striking of cue ball at 3 o'clock very important.

With practice and as your knowledge of angles improves, this very difficult shot will become more consistently easy to attain.

23 — Railroad Five Shot

DESCRIPTION: The intention here is to pocket the red ball into the centre pocket for 3, and complete the 5 shot by making a cannon via the cues to the opponent's white ball.

TO SET UP: Place three cues into pocket opening with all three balls positioned as shown.

HOW TO PLAY: Aim red ball into centre pocket as indicated by red line. At the same time cue ball will travel intended white line up into chute formed by the cues.

Cue ball will take the loop and return back along white line, meeting up with opponent's white ball to complete the 5 shot. This is a medium paced shot, striking cue ball above centre at 13.

SECOND PICTURE: Note cue ball has just taken the loop and is on the way down to meet up with the opponent's white ball.

MAIN POINTS: If the shot is played too soft, the cue ball will not mount the cues. If played too hard, it will go over the pocket.

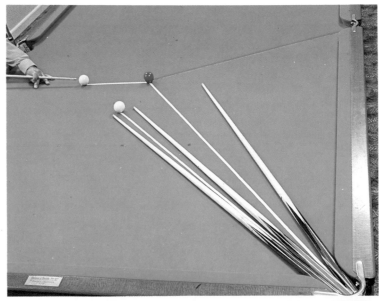

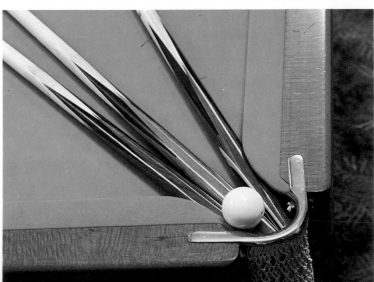

24 — Three Pocket Shot

DESCRIPTION: The pictures reveal the joke, and one that any ordinary billiard player can make.

TO SET UP: Place red and white balls on drop of each corner pocket. Place two cues together touching as well as touching both balls.

HOW TO PLAY: Strike cue ball dead centre down table over spots with a hard stroke.

Cue ball will rebound up the table, over the spots to strike the cues above the black spot.

Cue ball should have sufficient speed on striking cue to bounce into the air, over the end cushion, where player catches ball and places it into the unexpected third pocket. Impact on to cues is responsible for pocketing both red and white in the same shot.

MAIN POINTS: Striking cue ball dead centre, applying power to the shot, will ensure that the cue ball travelling down the table over the spots will return back up the table over the spots.

Fast speed is essential to get the cue ball into the air and over end cushion rail after impact on to the two cues.

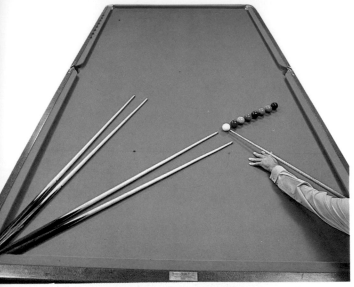

25 — The Rapid Firing Steeplechase Shot

DESCRIPTION: This fast action shot has all the colours chasing each other around the angles to line up for the chute and the top pocket.

TO SET UP: The butts of all four cues are jammed evenly into the pocket jaws just past the fall of the slate. Nameplates on both inside cues to face one another so that each pair of cues can be angled out, thus widening the entrance to the chute. All 8 coloured balls are lined up at the barrier as shown 13 mm (½″) apart.

HOW TO PLAY: Strike cue ball, aiming at first red marker from centre pocket shown on side cushion. All 8 balls are sent to their corresponding marker all the way down side cushion. Black will strike final marker at top of side cushion. Strike all balls dead centre with medium to hard strength.

SECOND PICTURE: The balls are on the move, with the white having travelled 3 cushions heading for the chute, followed by the red just leaving the third cushion, the yellow just leaving the second cushion, and the green approaching the first cushion.

THIRD PICTURE: Both white and red balls have already disappeared into intended pocket. Yellow ball is up in the chute, green is just entering the chute, brown is approaching into the other side of the chute, blue is just approaching the third cushion, pink is just leaving the second cushion, while black is still approaching the first cushion.

MAIN POINTS: Strike all balls dead centre to ensure against miscueing. With practice your speed of stroke will increase. Timing is essential to have all balls at one stage of the shot on the move. Practise this shot till your timing is such that the cue ball is in the chute with all balls following and the black having just commenced its journey from the cue.

26 – Blue, Pink and Black to Win

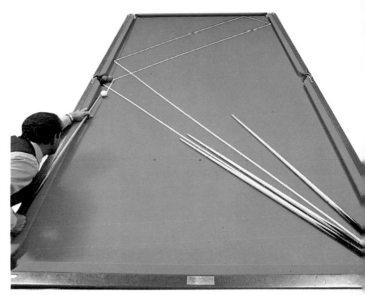

DESCRIPTION: If ever you are confronted with this extremely difficult-looking shot and requiring blue, pink and black to win, don't muck about; you can finish the game in one shot.

TO SET UP: Blue ball is on the fall and middle of centre pocket.

Pink ball touching blue is aimed across table to opposite centre pocket.

Cue ball 20 cm (8″) from pink and the width of one ball out from cushion.

Black is over centre pocket, nearer to the side cushion jaw, and clear of blue and pink.

HOW TO PLAY: Aim cue ball one-third on to right side of pink ball, striking cue ball at 10 o'clock.

Pink will chip blue into centre pocket, continuing on down red line into corner pocket.

Cue ball will travel white line around the angles up into the chute, around the railway loop and on down the cues finally pocketing black ball into centre pocket.

MAIN POINTS: Correct contact on to pink, as described, is most important, as is striking cue ball at 10 o'clock. Strength of stroke has to be near perfect for this shot. If the shot is underhit, the cue ball will not have sufficient pace to mount the cues and take the loop. If overhit, the cue ball will travel into the chute too fast, over the top of the pocket brass and off the table.

27 — The Shunting Shot

DESCRIPTION: Shunting all seven balls into centre pocket. This is a very pretty and popular trick shot which can be fairly easily mastered.

TO SET UP: Place two cues touching 40 cm (16″) out from the centre pocket with the inside cue 8 cm (3″) shorter than the outside one.

Mount all seven balls, as shown in photo one, up on the butts of the two cues.

HOW TO PLAY: Place your right hand on the white ball in the form of a brake, releasing each front ball at 20 cm (8″) intervals.

Balls will roll on down the cues gaining momentum, turning off the cues to the left when dropping off the tip of the inside cue in the direction of the centre pocket.

SECOND PICTURE: Shows all balls shunting off down the line with yellow almost ready to enter the centre pocket and the green ready to come off the cues.

MAIN POINTS: After some practice you will learn to position cues at the right distance and right angle out from intended centre pocket, so that balls enter pocket. When placing balls on to cue butts, and while aligning balls to shunt on down, be careful not to allow any movement of either cue.

28 — The Magician

DESCRIPTION: Pocketing red ball from under handkerchief leaving the cue ball on the handkerchief.

TO SET UP: Place red ball near brown spot covered by and under centre of handkerchief. Flatten out all edges of handkerchief.

HOW TO PLAY: Aim white at mound made by red ball.

Strike cue ball at 15 with a hard stroke.

Result will be that red ball will come from under handkerchief on red line as shown to pocket, cue ball will stop on handkerchief.

SECOND PICTURE: Shows the red ball heading into corner pocket and cue ball stopped on handkerchief.

MAIN POINTS: Place red under centre of outstretched handkerchief. Make a straight pot of the cue ball under the mound of the handkerchief and the pocket. Strike the mound full. Speed will be required not only to stun the cue ball to an abrupt halt on the centre of the handkerchief, but also for the red ball to force from under the laid-out handkerchief at sufficient speed to keep it on its path to the pocket.

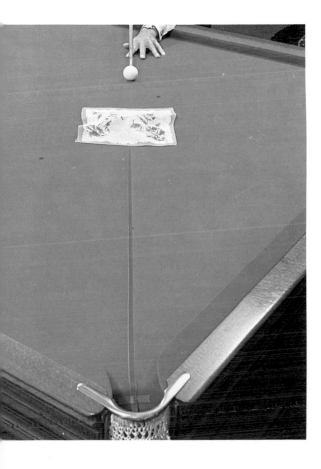
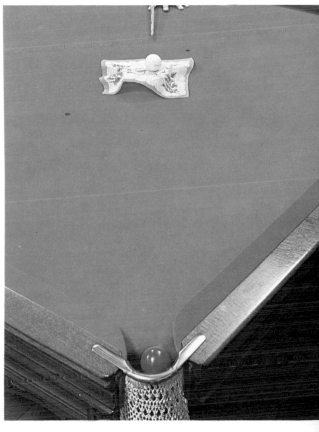

29 – Ball in the Basket

DESCRIPTION: This might be a shot for experts but it won't harm you to try it. All that is required is for the ball to be jumped over the reds and into the neck of the basket.

TO SET UP: Place cane basket on centre of table.

Place three pairs of reds blocking the path to the basket as shown.

Cue ball 10 cm (4″) out from cushion.

HOW TO PLAY: Raise your cue butt.

Play down on to cue ball at 12 o'clock with a really forceful stroke.

Cue ball will pass over reds and into the basket as per picture two.

MAIN POINTS: Power is needed to get the cue ball to jump, but at the same time the cue ball must be struck high with an elevated cue butt. Although the basket opening is very near in size to the cue ball, it is amazing how quickly you learn to strike at the right speed to continually get the cue ball into the basket, or another (non-breakable) vessel of your choice.

134

30 — Blue Ball Out

DESCRIPTION: This is an even more ambitious version of the previous shot, as it aims to spin the basket with the cue ball and throw out the concealed blue ball.

TO SET UP: Here you see the balls placed in a similar position as for forcing the cue ball over the reds and into the basket. On this occasion, however, the blue has been placed in the basket and the basket turned so that the opening has been reduced to half.

HOW TO PLAY: Again, by applying a very forceful stroke with the cue butt raised, the intention is to force the cue ball through the air over the reds and into the basket on the full. With the basket opening being at an angle to the cue ball, the cue ball will hit inside the neck of the cane basket. This spins the basket and throws the blue ball out. The cue ball will stay in.

MAIN POINTS: Strike the cue ball at 12 o'clock and remember it is a power shot. Accurate aim is called for here as it is one of the most difficult trick shots of all, getting the cue ball through the air for a distance of approximately six feet into the half-closed opening of the basket.

31 — Tumble Shot

DESCRIPTION: The idea here is to tip up the basket to pocket the red in its centre pocket, at the same time pocketing the blue back into the opposite centre pocket.

TO SET UP: Place basket upright with opening covering blue spot.

Place blue ball in the centre and bottom of the basket against the lip and the red ball on the drop of the opposite centre pocket.

HOW TO PLAY: Cue ball, neck of basket and red ball are all on line.

Strike cue ball dead centre a hard stroke.

Cue ball will pass through neck of basket to pocket the red.

Blue ball will be thrown from the tumbling basket back into opposite centre pocket, as shown, in second picture.

MAIN POINTS: Do not raise the cue butt any higher than you have to in cueing over the side cushion as it is important to keep the cue ball down on the bed cloth.

Correct placing of basket on blue spot and blue ball as shown on basket are the main essentials to accomplishing this very attractive trick shot.

32 — Double Kissing Shot

DESCRIPTION: Pocket the red, before making cannon and in-off.

TO SET UP: Place red ball hard on jaw of the corner pocket as shown.
   Cue ball 20 cm (8″) from red ball.
   Opponent's white is out from middle of centre pocket width of a ball.

HOW TO PLAY: Aim cue ball full on to red ball, striking cue ball at 6 o'clock a medium strength stroke.
   Cue ball will double kiss off red, pocketing red into corner pocket for 3.
   Cue ball will return back along side cushion as shown by white line making contact on to opponent's white ball for 2, before dropping into pocket for 3 thus completing the 8 shot.

MAIN POINTS: The correct contact of cue ball on to red ball and 6 o'clock striking of the cue ball are very important. Try to feel this stroke as it really is a touch shot.

33 – A Forcing Eight Shot

DESCRIPTION: Using the length and breadth of the table and a bit of swerve we must aim to pocket red and cannon the white, before final in-off.

TO SET UP: Place red ball hard on pocket jaw. Opponent's white ball just off the point and out 13 mm (½″) from side cushion jaw. Cue ball on green spot.

HOW TO PLAY: Play a forceful stroke striking cue ball at 1 o'clock to strike just below red on side cushion as indicated by white line.

White to rebound, catching red half ball on right side where the double kiss will pocket red.

Cue ball will bounce across and out before top spin takes effect and swings the cue ball back into the top cushion before rebounding to opponent's white ball and making the in-off to the corner pocket.

Result: An extremely fine 8 shot.

MAIN POINTS: Strike cue ball at 1 o'clock with force. Catching the red the correct thickness of contact is all important, both in pocketing the red and having the cue ball swing out from that contact before top spin takes it back across the table.

The shot will require much practice.

34 — In-Off on the Run

DESCRIPTION: A bit of timing is needed here as you roll the red ball down the table and play an in-off the red while it is on the run.

TO SET UP: Play from baulk end with the red ball and the cue ball in your left hand. The red ball is between thumb and forefinger, with cue ball held in the palm of your hand and remaining fingers.

HOW TO PLAY: Roll red at medium strength down the table as shown in picture one. Watch red ball all the way down till it reaches an area adjacent to the pink spot, as shown in picture two.

While that is happening, place cue ball on or near the baulk line and align your stance to quickly fire the cue ball after the red, as indicated by white line. Score in-off into top left corner pocket, driving red around the table as indicated by red line.

MAIN POINTS: Practice will certainly be required for these moving ball shots.

I play this shot these days with virtually 100% consistency by throwing the red on line just to the left of the pink spot and watching the red all the time. While the red is travelling down to the pink spot (and I have sent it down with some force), I have placed the cue ball, aligned my cue behind the white and without watching the cue ball (I can see it out of the corner of my eye), I send the cue ball after the red, thus catching it before it virtually travels 8 cm (3″), to make the desired contact.

Aim to contact the red between three-quarters and half ball on left side.

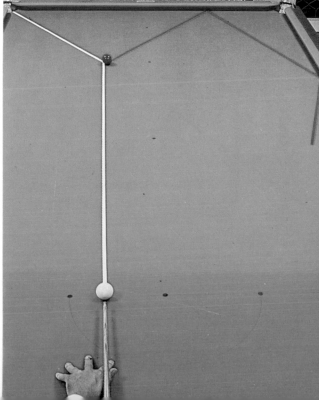

35 — Pocketing Red on the Run

DESCRIPTION: Another moving shot, this time aiming to pocket the object ball.

TO SET UP: Hold red and cue ball as explained in previous shot.

Throw red, however, to opposite side of pink spot for this shot.

Send cue ball racing after red to make red in right top corner pocket.

HOW TO PLAY: Allow red to reach area adjacent to right of pink spot as shown in picture two. Follow red with your eyes from your hand, all the way up the table. Send white after red using the same system as last shot. Again aim white to left side of red, half to three-quarters full, this time however to send red off on red line to pocket as shown. Cue ball will follow white line.

MAIN POINTS: It is a more difficult shot to pot the red than to go in-off while balls are moving. Get your eyes behind the line of the red from the time it leaves your left hand. Timing your cue ball to reach the red is the main essential. If you are to become proficient at this trick shot you must practice.

36 — Cannon — Two Balls Moving

DESCRIPTION: This time a pot and a cannon from moving balls, with the white racing behind to catch up with red, pocketing red ball off to the right top pocket, with the cue ball continuing on around five cushions to complete the cannon on to your opponent's white ball.

HOW TO PLAY: Hold red and cue ball as previously explained.

Throw red down the table on a line to the left of centre spots.

Allow red to reach approximately 30 cm (12″) above centre pocket.

While red is travelling to that position, place cue ball and strike white 2 o'clock.

Catch red three-quarters full on left side with sufficient speed for cue ball to travel white line as shown, thus completing the 5 shot.

SECOND PICTURE: I have my shot away, cue ball has made contact with red. Red is now moving towards corner pocket and cue ball continues its journey around 5 cushions to meet up with opponent's white ball.

MAIN POINTS: A really tough shot to make, but it is one of my favourites.

Excellent timing is called for here. Follow the red ball with your eyes from the time it leaves your hand. Concentrate on catching red 36-41 cm (14-16″) above centre pocket.

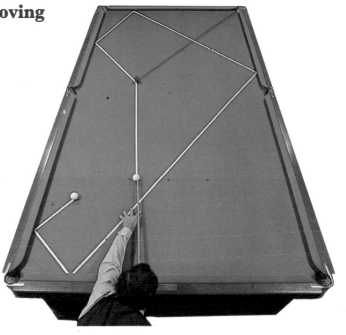

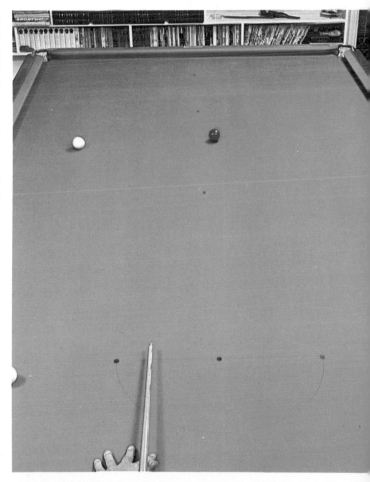

37 — Chaser Cannon

DESCRIPTION: Racing all three balls around the angles to make a cannon into the bottom left corner of the table. A very clever shot, but the possible combination of cannons in the top corner allows some margin for error.

TO SET UP: Line three billiard balls 2.5 cm (1″) apart near baulk line.

HOW TO PLAY: Send first white with a medium stroke to marker as indicated on first side cushion. That ball will continue on white line as shown, as will red and finally second white.

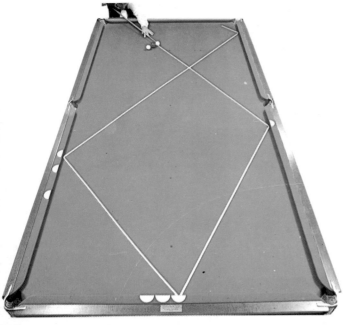

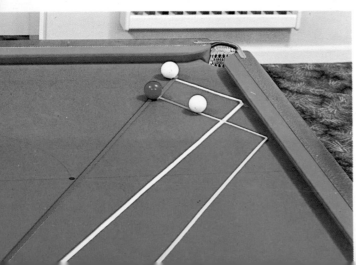

Red ball if sent racing to same first marker, will return to second cushion striking face of cushion at middle white marker as shown, carrying on to middle white marker on opposite side of table and on up into corner.

Second white ball, if aimed to first white marker, will travel to second cushion to outside left marker as shown and on to closest white marker indicated on opposite side cushion before travelling on approximately the same line as the previous 2 balls into the desired area.

There are many combinations for making this chaser cannon into the corner of the table indicated.

Second picture shows just one of those many combinations where first white following white line shown has travelled closest to corner pocket. Red ball, having followed angle explained, will be approaching that white ball on red line.

Second white ball having approached first two balls into corner of table along yellow line as shown, because of greater speed, will catch red and cannon off on to first white as shown by blue lines illustrated.

MAIN POINTS: Strike all three balls dead centre with cue tip. Strike first white ball at medium strength, allowing it to have reached approximately midway between the first and second cushions before striking red a harder stroke at a speed that will allow it to catch the first white in the bottom left corner of the table, where the cannon will take place.

Having allowed the first white ball to have left the third cushion and the red ball the second cushion, send the second white ball at high speed. Red ball is slowing down allowing the second white to first catch the red before making a cannon on to first white.

38 — The Blue Flyer

DESCRIPTION: Announce here that your intention is to strike the blue ball before touching either red.

TO SET UP: Place reds touching against bottom cushion.

Balance blue on edge of bottom cushion resting on both reds, cue ball near pink spot.

HOW TO PLAY: Cue vigorously at the ball, indicating that you are going to really clout the cue ball with a very hard stroke. However, finally strike cue ball with only sufficient strength to reach reds.

Allow cue ball to reach approximately the baulk line before slapping your end cushion a hard blow with the flat of your hand.

The vibration will force blue, already delicately balancing in its position, to spread the two reds and drop down on to table in the path of oncoming white ball for the desired contact to take place, as shown in picture two.

MAIN POINTS: Not much to remember here as cue ball can be struck dead centre. Timing the slap of your hand on to the cushion rail is important. The blue should drop down at absolutely the last second to meet the approaching cue ball.

143

39 — Kissing the Blue into the Centre Pocket

DESCRIPTION: I will play off the red so that the cue ball will cross the table and hit the opposite side cushion, returning across the table in the direction of the centre pocket. Meanwhile the blue ball will be travelling up the side cushion where I intend to meet up with it and kiss it into the centre pocket.

TO SET UP: Place red and blue touching hard on side cushion, approximately 40 cm (16″) out from corner pocket.

Cue ball 5 cm (2″) from red closer to corner pocket, also touching side cushion.

HOW TO PLAY: Picture two shows cue ball has played off the side of red across the table to side cushion, to return across the table where I had led my audience to believe it was going to meet up with the blue and kiss it into the centre pocket.

Blue has travelled down blue line as shown and red has cut out on short red line as shown. When it becomes quite obvious that I have played the cue ball too far in advance of the blue, pick up the blue, kiss it and drop it into the centre pocket.

MAIN POINTS: Strike cue ball dead centre with sufficient strength for white to travel across table to side cushion and back across table, while blue has travelled approximately on a line out between centre pockets.

While walking down the side of the table to catch up on the blue, time yourself so that about the time it becomes obvious to the majority of your audience that you have in fact sent the cue ball too far ahead of the blue for any contact to ever take place, exclaim to your audience: 'How am I going this time?', hopefully to draw the remark: 'You've missed'. At this point pick up the blue ball while it is still travelling past the centre pocket, kiss the blue, and drop it with your hand into the centre pocket!

40 — Over and Under

DESCRIPTION: This shot will take the cue ball over the spider and score six by potting the red and drawing back for an in-off.

TO SET UP: Place spider as shown with red ball 5 cm (2″) from handle of spider on player's side. Cue ball 20 cm (8″) from red.

HOW TO PLAY: Strike cue ball at 6 o'clock with a raised cue butt.

Apply a power shot.

Aim red full to centre of opposite pocket where it will travel red line.

Cue ball struck with power will be in the air when it reaches red.

Impact on to red ball will force cue ball to hurdle over spider handle.

On coming down to bed cloth on opposite side of spider handle, back spin will draw cue ball back under handle on white line shown in to pocket immediately in front of player.

MAIN POINTS: Sufficient power for cue ball to only just climb over the spider handle is the essential thing. If sent too high in the air, on coming down on to the bed cloth, the cue ball will have a tendency to bounce, and back spin will be lost. A difficult shot to play but a very cute shot once mastered.

41 — The Kangaroo Hop — Ten Shot

DESCRIPTION: Here, with the help of the cushion rail, you can pocket the red, cannon, pot your opponent's white and go in-off. You will pocket the red into corner pocket for 3, jump cue ball up on to end cushion and back on to opponent's white for 5. Opponent's cue ball will drop into corner pocket for 7, with player's cue ball following to complete the 10 shot.

TO SET UP: Place red ball 2.5 cm (1″) out from face at bottom cushion.

Cue ball 15 cm (6″) from red to white marker on bottom cushion just to left of corner pocket.

HOW TO PLAY: With raised cue butt, strike cue ball at 6 o'clock, aiming red at corner pocket along red line as shown.

With a short, brisk stroke cue ball will hurdle up on to cushion.

Strong back spin will draw white quickly back, on white line as shown, to meet opponent's white ball, cannoning opponent's white ball for five, pocketing opponent's white ball for seven with player's cue ball following on into the pocket to complete the 10 shot.

MAIN POINTS: Striking cue ball at 6 o'clock with a highly raised cue butt at just the right speed is absolutely vital to getting the cue ball high enough to land on the cushion without carrying on over the cushion and off the table.

This is a highly skilful shot. It is one of my own trick shots and an audience favourite. Many tables will not have cushion rails to suit this shot, as the cue ball could perhaps roll off the cushion back on to the table bed or carry on over the cushion rail. The cushion needs to be perfectly level with the wooden rail slightly above the cloth, thus forming an edge for the cue ball to run against.

42 — Machine-gun Shot

DESCRIPTION: This is, perhaps, one of the best known trick shots in Australia, as it is used in the opening titles of the ABC TV show *Super Snooker*. It is not so much a trick shot as a spectacular shot requiring perfect cueing. The intention is to send the white ball slowly towards the corner pocket, racing it in with all 7 object balls. The white ball is sent on its way first, but goes in last.

TO SET UP: Line all 8 balls across the baulk line as shown with black on green spot and remaining balls just clear of one another.

HOW TO PLAY: Strike all balls dead centre. Aim cue ball to white marker on end cushion to right of pocket, looking back from camera.

Play white ball with sufficient strength to only comfortably reach the corner pocket.

Coming across and into the nap on most tables will turn white ball as it slows down on its journey to pocket so you must allow for this by aiming at white marker. Having started white ball on its journey, quickly move across (bridge hand should never leave the table) and get red on its way with some power, quickly followed by yellow, then green and so on. Black ball has to make corner pocket comfortably ahead of white ball.

FIRST PICTURE: The balls line up as explained.

SECOND PICTURE: The white ball is on its journey with red, yellow and green already on the way and I am preparing to move across to strike the brown.

THIRD PICTURE: The red has reached the brink of the pocket quickly followed by yellow, green, brown, blue and I am about to strike the pink. I am going to have plenty of time to race the white ball in finally with the black.

MAIN POINTS: On lining this shot up, make sure all balls have sufficient clearance past one another to the pocket. Strike all balls dead centre. Immediately get across and rattle the red and yellow, in particular, at fast speed towards the pocket before they are cut off by the white ball. As you move across the table and having commenced the first couple of balls on their journey, you can begin to slow down as each ball in turn has a shorter journey to travel to the pocket.

On the last picture, played on the move, my timing is near perfect. By the time I strike the black, red and yellow will have disappeared into the pocket, green, brown, blue and pink will all have moved closer to pocket leaving me a comparatively simple task of getting the black in behind the pink ahead of the white.

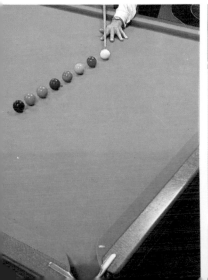

43 — Blue, Pink and Black to Win — One Shot

DESCRIPTION: Having been confronted recently with this shot requiring blue, pink and black to win, I decided to get the game over in a hurry with one shot.

TO SET UP: Place the blue in the vicinity of brown spot. Place black and pink touching over blue spot and on line to centre pockets.

HOW TO PLAY: Fire blue ball into centre pocket, at the same time bringing cue down between pink and black thus spreading them into each centre pocket.

MAIN POINTS: Move quickly in making this shot but be careful that in your anxiety to impress your audience that you don't break your favourite cue!

44 -- Four Balls, Four Pockets -- One Shot

DESCRIPTION: This time I am going to pocket the yellow, green, brown and blue in that order into four different pockets, all in the one shot.

TO SET UP: Place brown ball over bottom left corner pocket, yellow ball over left centre pocket, green ball over top left corner pocket, blue ball over right centre pocket, cue ball adjacent to green spot.

Three touching reds to be placed against yellow in a straight line to blue.

Two reds planted straight at brown to 20 cm (8″) out from side cushion and 20 cm (8″) out from end cushion.

HOW TO PLAY: The idea here is to strike the cue ball at 6 o'clock drawing it off centre red, cannoning on to red near yellow, before cue ball hits side cushion to return across table and out of the way.

Red near yellow will chip yellow into pocket and travel on down side rail to pocket green. Centre red will drive up table to top cushion, return down table to hit front red so that back red will pot brown.

Finally outside red will cross table and pocket blue. A hard stroke is a must.

PICTURE ONE: The picture shows the situation I am confronted with, with me at the end of the table explaining the shot.

PICTURE TWO: I am at the address with cue tip at 6 o'clock aiming cue ball to centre red as shown by white line.

MAIN POINTS: Striking point on cue ball 6 o'clock. Aim at centre red half a ball on left side and play with a hard stroke. Outside red will slowly cross the table to pocket blue, so a power shot is an absolute must.

It will follow on that yellow, green and brown will all be pocketed, provided the red balls adjacent to yellow have been set up as described.

45 — Blue, Pink and Black to Win

DESCRIPTION: Another way of getting blue, pink and black down in one 'trick shot'.

TO SET UP: Place black on pink spot.

Position blue so that black is planted to red marker on side cushion just to left of corner pocket.

Both balls should be touching.

Place pink in centre of top left corner pocket.

Cue ball 5 cm (2″) in from yellow spot on baulk line.

HOW TO PLAY: Aim cue ball three-quarters full on left side of blue.

Strike cue ball at 12 o'clock.

Cue ball will play off blue to pocket pink.

Black will follow pink into same pocket.

Blue will plant off into opposite corner pocket.

MAIN POINTS: A medium to very firm stroke is required here to ensure black reaches pocket. Very gratifying to see all three coloured balls disappear, leaving only the cue ball on the table!

46 — Seven Balls in One Stroke

DESCRIPTION: Pocket all six 'over' pool balls in one centre pocket, and 8 ball in opposite centre pocket.

TO SET UP: Line six 'over' balls (9 to 15) all touching in straight line to centre pocket.
Place triangle against those six balls, point first.
Make sure back of triangle is square to cue ball.
Black to be positioned over opposite centre pocket.

HOW TO PLAY: Strike cue ball at 6 o'clock, a hard stroke, as cue ball will drive triangle into all six balls, pocketing them in Indian file fashion, while cue ball will rebound to pocket black.

MAIN POINTS: It is of utmost importance to get all balls placed on perfect line to ensure success with this shot.

47 – The Hurdle Shot

DESCRIPTION: To pocket the 8 ball out of the cluster from the side cushion through the triangle, over the balls into the bottom left corner pocket.

TO SET UP: Place black ball hard on side cushion just outside baulk line.

5 ball (orange) touching black and touching cushion.

1 ball (yellow) and 6 ball (green) are touching and are touching black and orange, thus forming a tight cluster.

Place cue ball 40 cm (16″) from orange ball and 15 cm (6″) out from side cushion.

Place triangle cushion-to-cushion across bottom left corner pocket.

Behind triangle place three balls blocking path to pocket.

HOW TO PLAY: Strike cue ball dead centre with power, full onto orange ball. Cluster will split open allowing black to bounce off side cushion along red line as shown to strike triangle as in second picture, bouncing up and over the intervening balls to drop into corner pocket.

MAIN POINTS: To allow black to come off the side cushion at the right angle to head for the corner pocket, cluster of balls may have to be moved back or forward on side cushion to find the correct position, depending on the table you are playing on.

This is a very spectacular shot and must be played with power to get the black up the table with sufficient force to go over the triangle and the obstructing balls to fall cleanly into the pocket.

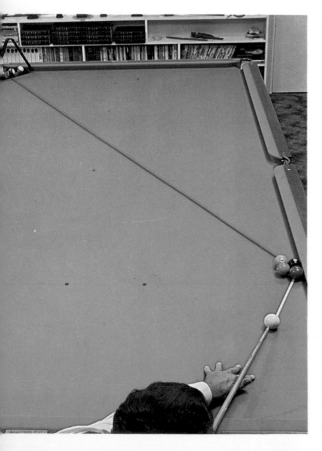

48 — Pocket Red and Handkerchief

DESCRIPTION: This time the handkerchief goes into the pocket with the red.

TO SET UP: Place red in vicinity of brown spot. Cover red with handkerchief, making sure red is three-quarter the way back from front edge of handkerchief.

HOW TO PLAY: Aim at mound under handkerchief as when trying to pot the red from under handkerchief as in earlier shot. Play with some power as red must wrap in handkerchief and carry handkerchief to corner pocket where it will go down with red ball.

MAIN POINTS: The secret of success here is to ensure that the handkerchief is positioned correctly. If it is not spread well in front of red (pocket side), red is sure to just come from under. Perseverance will pay off here in placing handkerchief and aiming at mound of red correctly.

49 – Paper Bag Shot

DESCRIPTION: Play the red ball into the paper bag, out of the paper bag, into the pocket.

TO SET UP: Place paper bag on line between blue spot and centre pockets one-third of the way out across table.

Place red ball 20 cm (8″) from bag with cue ball 20 cm (8″) from red.

Red, white and bag are all on line to centre pocket.

HOW TO PLAY: Strike cue ball below centre at 15 with below medium strength. Red ball will enter bag, flip bag over as shown in picture two and come back out the other side on way to pocket as shown in picture three.

MAIN POINTS: Cue at cue ball as if you were going to play this shot with tremendous power. The majority of your audience will think you are going to drive the red ball right through the paper bag. When the time comes to strike the cue ball, however, stop your cue action short and thus, at the absolute last second, actually play a delicate stroke so that the bag can very gracefully tumble over, with red entering centre pocket.

50 — Short Coin Shot

DESCRIPTION: Just for a change dispense with balls and try your luck firing a 20c coin into the centre pocket.

TO SET UP: Place coin under cushion leaning top into side cushion.

HOW TO PLAY: Strike the coin with the cue tip a softish stroke, allowing coin to head out from cushion where angle of coin will keep the coin falling back into the cushion. Coin may bounce against cushion 4 to 5 times before getting to centre pocket, where it will drop in.

MAIN POINTS: It is the angle on the coin and the correct strength of stroke that will be responsible for making this shot. It is a very pretty little shot, and with practice not a difficult shot to play.

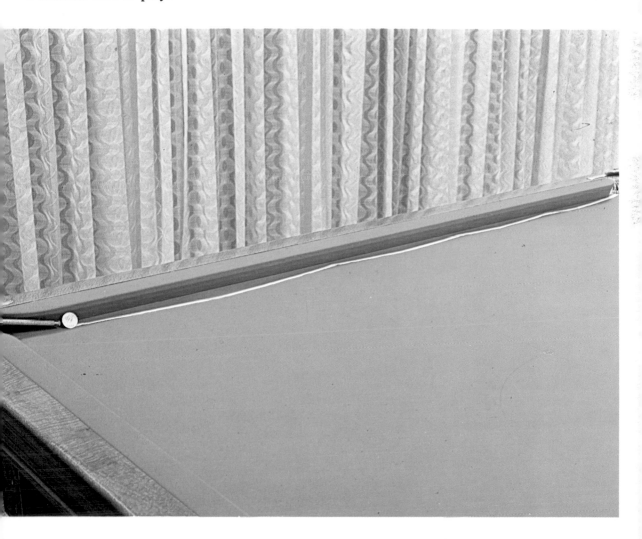

51 — Long Coin Shot

DESCRIPTION: Fire coin down side cushion to top pocket.

TO SET UP: Place the coin tilting top of coin into the cushion.

HOW TO PLAY: Play a firm stroke sending the coin out 20-25 cm (8-10″) wide of the centre pocket. As the force of the stroke subsides, the coin will arc back towards the corner pocket because of the tilt originally arranged.

Coin may brush side cushion once or twice before disappearing into corner pocket.

MAIN POINTS: Again, arranging the correct tilt to the coin is extremely important. Striking the coin with the right strength of stroke will keep it travelling on its edge the full 370 cm (12′) of the table. If underhit the coin will fall over flat before reaching the pocket, and if carelessly overhit, it can bounce over, skidding to a stop far short of the corner pocket.

52 — The Flip Shot

DESCRIPTION: This is quite a classy shot, which aims to pocket the coin into the glass.

TO SET UP: Place a 10c coin on the cushion rubber 6 mm (¼″) back from the edge.

Place a small whisky glass on the back edge of the cushion immediately behind the coin.

Cue ball to be aligned as shown with the coin and glass.

HOW TO PLAY: Strike cue ball dead centre with a medium strength stroke, striking the cushion immediately in front of coin.

Coin will flip in the air as shown in picture two before falling into the glass.

MAIN POINTS: Playing this shot at the right speed is all important. Too soft a shot will not lift the coin sufficiently to achieve your purpose, whereas overhitting will result in the coin going right over the side rail and on to the floor.

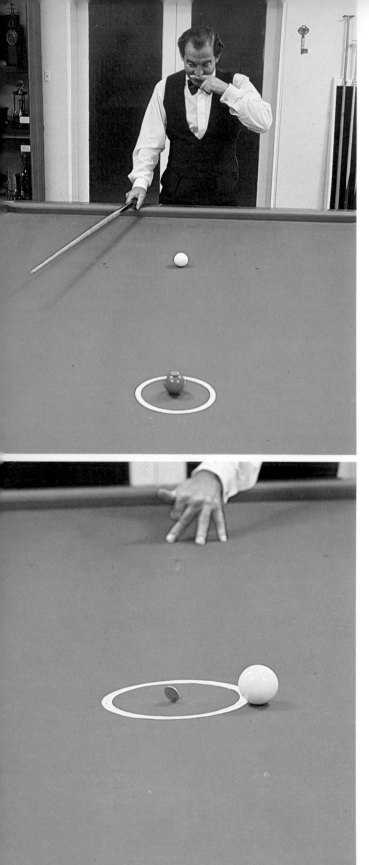

53 — The 'Impossible' Money Shot

DESCRIPTION: This is the trick shot I have most often 'suggested' to me by wags at the various places I play. The challenge is to play at the pink ball and to get the 10c coin on top of the pink ball out of the circle.

TO SET UP: Place pink on pink spot, cutting a white circle of paper to place evenly around the pink ball.

Place a 10c coin on top of pink ball.
Cue ball on brown spot.

THE PICTURES: Picture one shows the shot I am confronted with.

Picture two shows an unsuccessful shot. I have certainly cleared the pink and white out of the circle, but the coin, as so often happens, has remained inside. Try it yourself a few times and I bet that you, too, are unsuccessful.

Then, to learn the correct way to play this shot, turn to page 175.

54 — Two Reds in One Shot

DESCRIPTION: A fancy way of pocketing two reds in the one shot, by going the long way round.

TO SET UP: Place one red ball in the middle of the table 2.5 cm (1″) out from the bottom cushion, second red over the bottom left corner pocket. Cue ball 46 cm (18″) from red as shown.

HOW TO PLAY: Aim cue ball at red three-quarters full on right side, striking cue ball at 11 o'clock — a power stroke.

Red ball will rebound off bottom cushion, to side cushion, top cushion, side cushion as shown by red line to eventually enter the corner pocket.

Cue ball, meanwhile, has run through first red, making contact with second red to pocket that ball, thus leaving the way clear for second red returning from a world tour.

MAIN POINTS: Correct contact of cue tip on to cue ball and cue ball on to first red ball are the keys to making this shot.

55 — Flying 'White Horse' Shot

DESCRIPTION: A very clever shot which will require much practice. Here we find the White Horse covering the yellow, thus snookering the white. We have to send the cue ball flying over the stand and through the horse's legs to pocket the yellow.

TO SET UP: Place the horse, or your own suitable object, approximately in the middle of the table. Cue ball as shown and yellow ball into the mouth of the top corner pocket.

HOW TO PLAY: Again, as in all jump shots, address cue ball high at 12 o'clock with a raised cue butt. Strength of stroke is the all important thing.

Unlike most of my other jump shots there is a limit here on how high I can lift the cue ball because it must pass over the stand, but under its girth.

As the horse is 150 cm (5′) from cue ball, near perfect timing and strength of stroke are required. Go clean through the opening to pocket the yellow.

The second picture shows the cue ball still in the air after flying through the opening, probably at a speed in excess of over 100 k.p.h. and racing towards the yellow.

MAIN POINTS: Strike cue ball high with near perfect aim. Perfect cueing is called for to make a success of this shot.

56 — The Flying 'Swan' Shot

DESCRIPTION: The aim is to play a cannon off the yellow on to the red without touching the bottle. I can play this shot repeatedly, sometimes brushing the neck of the bottle with the cue ball in contacting red without ever knocking the bottle over.

TO SET UP: Place cue ball 10 cm (4″) out from end cushion.

Yellow ball 20 cm (8″) from white.

Place bottle just to player's right side of a straight line between white and yellow. Place a red ball on to opening of bottle.

HOW TO PLAY: Strike cue ball at 12 o'clock with a raised cue butt playing down on to cue ball with a medium strength stroke. Aim full at yellow ball.

White ball will strike yellow having risen from cloth (as in all jump shots). On making contact with yellow, cue ball will bounce higher.

Yellow ball will pass bottle on right looking back from camera.

Cue ball will lift red from bottle on contact.

Picture two shows cue ball having just cleared red so that it is falling back on my side of the bottle. Normally it will drop red on opposite side of bottle. However the bottle was not disturbed.

Wow! Note my expression! Who said trick shots were easy?

MAIN POINTS: This is not a forceful stroke. Stroked at the correct speed, the cue ball will catch the red gently at the top of its climb. The technique is to lift the white quickly from the yellow so that it is climbing virtually straight up when it contacts red.

If the bottle is placed too close on line with the white and yellow, the yellow ball will make contact on bottle, knocking it over or, in most cases, bursting the bottle.

A great shot to entertain your friends and should you make it first shot, celebrate by having a nice, cool glass of Swan!

57 — The 'Crown' Shot

DESCRIPTION: This shot looks fraught with disaster and you may be deterred by the thought of all that beer on the cloth. You have to pocket the two reds immediately in front of glass into each top corner pocket.

TO SET UP: Place cue ball 15 cm (6″) out from bottom cushion in front of nameplate.
Place 3 pairs of reds, as shown, between cue ball and baulk line.
Triangle outside of baulk line.
Red closest to glass on pink spot touching red furthest away from glass that is planting red ball on pink spot to left side cushion jaw just to left of pocket.
Beer glass containing beautiful frothy lager 2.5 cm (1″) behind above planted red balls.

HOW TO PLAY: Strike cue ball 12 o'clock with raised cue butt.
Cue ball will hurdle over reds and through triangle catching closest of planted balls full.
Closest red will plant off into right top pocket, other red to top left pocket.
The second picture shows red balls on way to respective pockets, with the glass untouched.

MAIN POINTS: If your aim is good and your hand is steady, don't worry about the glass — just imagine it isn't there. After all it could be a mirage!
Apply power. Cue ball should bounce only once after clearing triangle and will be down running level on bed when it contacts first of planted red balls. Although the glass is immediately behind reds, contact from either red or cue ball is impossible.
A great trick shot that could prove devastating! After making this one, drink the glass of Carlton Draught straight down the hatch — you'll have earned it!

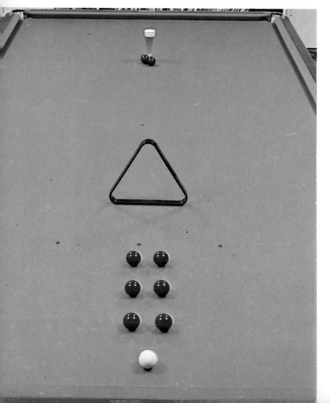

58 – The Hustler

DESCRIPTION: If you are true to the name of this shot you should take any bets on whether you can pocket the yellow from this seemingly 'impossible' set up.

TO SET UP: Make a half circle of touching red balls as shown around the green spot.

Place single red touching yellow 10 cm (4″) from first red on string of half circle reds and closest to player.

Plant yellow from single red just to left of corner pocket, looking back from camera, as indicated by yellow marker.

HOW TO PLAY: Strike cue ball at 7 o'clock, aiming one-third full to left of first red forming half circle.

Play with medium strength.

Cue ball will follow white line as shown cannoning off first red in half circle on to single red and out as indicated.

Yellow ball will follow yellow line to corner pocket.

Impact of cue ball on to first red forming half circle will start a chain reaction that will have cleared the reds so that path of yellow ball to pocket is unhindered.

MAIN POINTS: The secret of success here is to correctly position all balls as described.

59 — Pocketing a Ball Not On

DESCRIPTION: I must try to pocket the yellow into the corner pocket, when it is obstructed by the red ball.

TO SET UP: Place red ball **36** cm (**14"**) out from corner pocket hard up on end cushion.
Yellow ball half a ball out from cushion is touching red.
Cue ball behind brown spot 20 cm (8").

HOW TO PLAY: Aim cue ball at the yellow.
Strike cue ball at **6** o'clock with power.
Yellow ball will force red out along red line as shown leaving path clear for yellow ball to follow yellow line into pocket.

MAIN POINTS: Aim full at yellow, low on white with plenty of power. It is the heavy back spin applied to the cue ball that shunts the yellow ball forward after its spin has weakened. A real beauty!

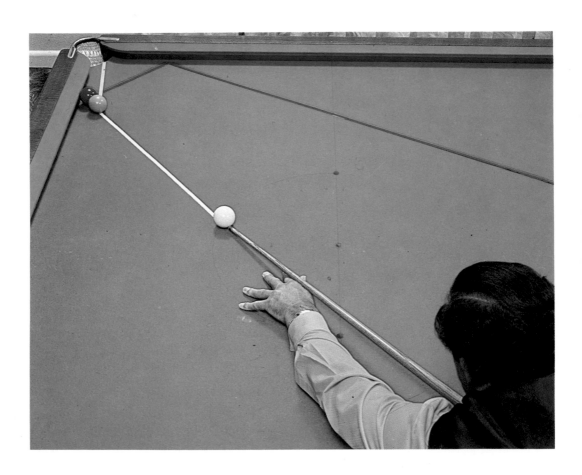

60 — The Piggy Back Shot

DESCRIPTION: This piggy back 8 shot will send the white and red down the table for a pocket with the red and an in-off your opponent's white.

TO SET UP: Place red ball hard against side cushion 20 cm (8″) out from pocket.

Cue ball up on cushion edge resting on red, opponent's white adjacent to opposite corner pocket as shown.

Aim red to centre of opposite corner pocket.

HOW TO PLAY: Strike cue ball dead centre with a slightly raised cue butt with medium strength stroke.

Aim cue ball half a ball to right of opponent's white ball (left side looking back from camera).

Red ball will travel red line to pocket behind cue ball that will have travelled a little distance on top of red before passing over red to go in-off white ahead of red reaching pocket.

MAIN POINTS: Set this shot up carefully and, with a very smooth cue action, aim your cue ball at your opponent's white ball as advised. Smooth cueing for this shot is the main essential.

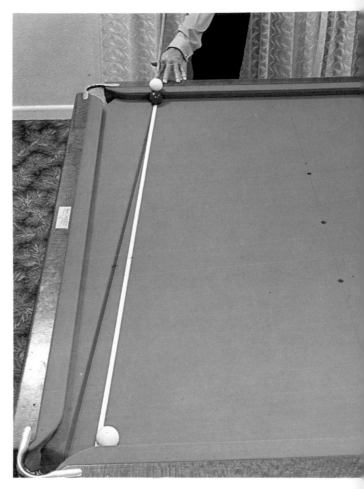

61 – Three Reds in One Shot

DESCRIPTION: A very intricate affair which will pocket all three reds into three separate pockets in one shot.

TO SET UP: Place blue ball on side cushion just before turn of pocket jaw with yellow touching blue planted to middle of opposite centre pocket.

Cue ball 30 cm (12") from yellow the width of one ball out from cushion as shown. One red over entrance to top left pocket, one over centre pocket and one over bottom right pocket.

HOW TO PLAY: Aim at yellow ball one-third full on right side.

Strike cue ball with medium to hard strength at 10 o'clock.

Yellow ball will travel yellow line to pocket red.

Blue ball will double across table along blue line to pocket centre red. Meanwhile cue ball to travel three cushions along white line as shown to pocket third and final red.

MAIN POINTS: It is important to place blue and yellow balls exactly as outlined. Strike cue ball at 10 o'clock, and with enough strength to allow the cue ball to travel its intended journey.

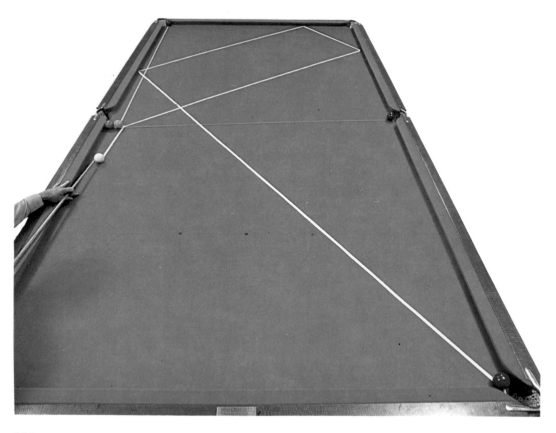

62 — The Red Kangaroo Shot

DESCRIPTION: This shot aims at jumping red out of the triangle into the centre pocket. The shot doesn't look possible, but it is attainable with practice.

TO SET UP: Place triangle as shown, red touching triangle making a line of red, point of triangle and blue spot on line to opposite centre pocket.

Cue ball 25 cm (10″) from red, lining red also to middle of opposite centre pocket.

HOW TO PLAY: Address cue ball high at 12 o'clock with a raised cue butt.

Play a medium strength stroke, aiming full at the red.

When played at the right speed, cue ball will jump just high enough to contact top of red, bouncing it out of the triangle (without touching) and into the opposite centre pocket.

Second picture shows red ball coming back to the bed cloth on line to the centre pocket after bounding out of triangle. Cue ball has moved over and ahead of red bouncing towards side cushion.

MAIN POINTS: As in all jump shots, address tip high to the cue ball. Strength of stroke must ensure rising the white to the red high enough in clearing triangle, but only at sufficient height to ensure contact on red ball.

63 – Draw Shot – Corner Pocket

DESCRIPTION: This is a legitimate billiards or snooker shot, but is spectacular enough to qualify as a trick shot as well. It is a deep screw shot which will draw a red back into corner pocket.

TO SET UP: Place red ball thickness of one ball out from side cushion, 30 cm (12″) from centre pocket.

Place cue ball at angle from red as shown 25cm (10″) from red.

HOW TO PLAY: Aim at red three-quarters full on left side of red.

Strike cue ball at 5 o'clock a medium to hard stroke.

Cue ball will draw back along white line as shown into corner pocket.

MAIN POINTS: Good cueing is called for. Correct contact on to red ball is most important, as is striking the cue ball at 5 o'clock. The side spin, combined with back spin on the cue ball by striking with a forceful stroke at 5 o'clock, will ensure the cue ball coming into the side cushion and kicking in-off the outside jaw as shown.

64 — Long Draw Shot

DESCRIPTION: The intention here is to pocket the red ball and draw the cue ball back and around two object balls as shown, eventually to pocket second red ball at bottom end of the table.

TO SET UP: Place red 2.5 cm (1″) out from side cushion 30 cm (12″) from corner pocket. Place white making red a straight pot.

HOW TO PLAY: Aim to strike red full, striking cue ball at 5 o'clock.

    Cue ball to screw right back along white line, as shown, where side spin combined with back spin on the cue ball will drift the cue ball (coming back into the nap) into the side cushion before meeting up with and pocketing second red.

MAIN POINTS: Again this is not a trick shot, but a very sweet fancy shot. Excellent cueing is the order of the day. Apply strength to this stroke as cue ball has a long way to travel.

65 — A Difficult Snooker

DESCRIPTION: I have been snookered on the yellow with one or two obstacles in the way!

Having been cut off with a direct stroke to the yellow by the reds, as shown, and with my very sweet next door neighbour, Melissa, having a grandstand seat in the centre of my table, I was left no alternative but to send the cue ball through the legs of the chair, around the angles as shown, passing back under the chair, missing all four legs to successfully pocket the yellow.

TO SET UP: Find your own friend, but not a heavy one, to take a seat close to the action. Arrange a circle of reds to cut off your shot to the yellow.

HOW TO PLAY: Strike cue ball at 12 o'clock a medium to hard stroke.

Cue ball will travel the angles as line indicates to yellow.

MAIN POINTS: With all respect to my photographer, editor and secretary, Melissa was the sweetest workmate I had in doing the entire book!

66 — Two Centre Pocket Reds

DESCRIPTION: We can pocket the two reds into the centre pocket with the blue and yellow in the way.

TO SET UP: Place first red over centre pocket and second red into area as shown.
   Place blue ball on line between two reds.
   Place yellow ball as shown.

HOW TO PLAY: Aim red to centre pocket as indicated by red line striking cue ball at 5 o'clock with a medium strength stroke.
   Play with a 'nippy' action, nipping the cue tip on to the cue ball at 5 o'clock with a short on-off action.

MAIN POINTS: The pocketing of the first red is not to be a straight shot. The angle to be set up should allow player to aim approximately three-quarters full on to left side of red, thus sending it along red line. It is this angle and the 'nippy' stroke applied to the cue ball that will first move the cue ball away from the angle of the pot after striking the first red towards the yellow. The 'nip' action will have the cue ball, when the initial skid away from the first red is spent, nipping back inside yellow, therefore around blue as shown, back to pocket second red.

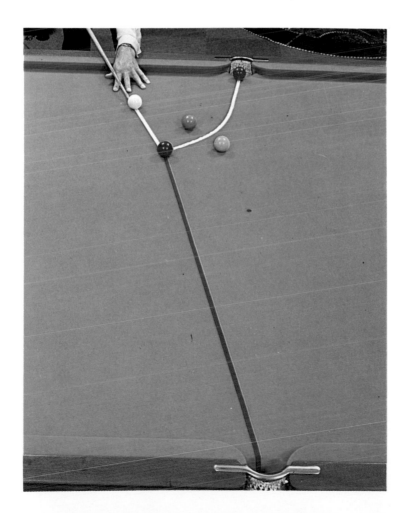

67 – The Pink Pearl

DESCRIPTION: We have to get the pink 'pearl' out of the pretty cluster of reds that protect it, and into the top left corner pocket, as indicated by yellow line.

TO SET UP: Place pink on its spot.

Cluster reds around pink so that both middle reds in each side cluster are touching pink.

End reds are touching centre red on each side.

Both openings between end reds on cluster are 13 mm (½″) wide.

Place cue ball on line of centre pocket and pink ball 30 cm (12″) out from centre pocket.

HOW TO PLAY: Strike cue ball a hard stroke at 15.

Aim cue ball to dead centre of first red as illustrated by white line.

Cue ball will spread reds as shown in picture three, where pink ball has commenced its journey towards intended corner pocket.

MAIN POINTS: The correct setting up as described is of utmost importance here. Picture one shows cue tip at 15 to send cue ball along white line, making full contact with nearest red to plant pink ball along yellow line as shown.

Picture two is a close up of the correctly assembled cluster. The red is the shell, the pink is the pearl.

Picture three shows an exploded view of the cluster immediately after impact of the cue ball.

68 — Three to Win

DESCRIPTION: Requiring three to win, don't bother playing a cannon with the task of scoring again, just play in-off the red without touching your opponent's white.

TO SET UP: Place red as shown just out from side cushion 25 cm (10″) from corner pocket.

Opponent's white is blocking path to pocket.

Cue ball 10 cm (4″) from red ball as shown.

HOW TO PLAY: Raise cue butt striking cue ball at 12 o'clock. Aim three-quarters full on left side of red ball and strike white with a firm stroke.

Cue ball will leave table slightly and, on contacting red, will lift further into the air, up and over opponent's white ball as shown in picture two, dropping cleanly into corner pocket.

MAIN POINTS: As in most jump shots, strike cue ball high at the correct speed to get required lift.

69 — Ten Shot

DESCRIPTION: A set up to pocket the red ball for three, make a cannon on to opponent's white for five, pocketing that white for seven and following in behind with cue ball to complete the ten shot.

TO SET UP: Place red over top left corner pocket.
Cue ball on green spot.
Oppponent's ball on brink of centre pocket.

HOW TO PLAY: Strike cue ball at 1 o'clock with force.
Aim cue ball to side cushion immediately below red ball as shown.
Cue ball to return from side cushion catching red half ball, pocketing same, moving from end cushion, across table to side cushion before returning finally to meet up with and pocket opponent's white ball.
If contact is right, player's cue ball, after catching opponent's white ball full, will follow it in.

MAIN POINTS: A very clever shot requiring much practice. Follow the instructions and practise until you pick the correct area of side cushion for ensuring correct contact on to red ball. When correct contact on to red is found, the rest will follow.

174

70 — Cannon and Righting the Basket

DESCRIPTION: With the basket in the way I aim to make a cannon and to up-end the basket so it stands the right way.

TO SET UP: Place neck of basket over pink spot.

    Red and white as shown above basket.

    Cue ball on brown spot.

HOW TO PLAY: Strike cue ball dead centre a hard stroke. Aim cue ball through neck of basket at the two balls behind basket.

    Picture two shows basket immediately after impact from cue ball beginning its half tumble.

    Picture three shows basket right way up with cannon complete.

MAIN POINTS: Exact speed of stroke the essential item here. The basket has to lift from the table at exactly the right speed, to land flat on its bottom so that it does not fall over.

Shot 53. THE SOLUTION: The way to get the coin out of the circle is to force it out. Address the cue ball at 12 o'clock with a raised cue butt and play full at pink with a lot of power.

The idea is for the cue ball to hurdle through the air and strike the pink on the full, thus hitting the coin at the same time.

Picture shows shot a fraction of a second after impact with the coin flying through the air.

MAIN POINTS: This is not a shot to play if you have had one too many to drink. It can become quite dangerous!

The Rules of Snooker

The General Rules, when not conflicting with any of the following Rules, govern this Game

Authorised by The Billiards and Snooker Control Council

<table>
<tr>
<td>DEFINITION
OF GAME</td>
<td>1.</td>
<td>The game of SNOOKER (or Snooker's Pool) is played on an English Billiard Table, and may be played by two or more persons, either as sides or independently. It is a game of winning hazards; cannons are ignored. The winner is the player or side making the highest score, or to whom the game under Rule 14 is awarded.</td>
</tr>
</table>

The Balls

<table>
<tr>
<td>NUMBER
IN SET</td>
<td>2.</td>
<td>The set of balls should be twenty-two in number, consisting of fifteen reds, one black, one pink, one blue, one brown, one green, one yellow, and a white ball, which is called the cue ball. In the game on the B. & S.C.C. 6' Standard Table the set of balls shall be seventeen in number, consisting of ten reds, one black, one pink, one blue, one brown, one green, one yellow, and a white ball, which is called the cue ball</td>
</tr>
</table>

Technical Terms

<table>
<tr>
<td></td>
<td>3. (a)</td>
<td>The white ball is referred to as the *cue ball;* the yellow, green, brown, blue, pink and black, as the *pool balls,* or *colours;* the red (or pyramid) balls, as *reds.*</td>
</tr>
<tr>
<td>BALL FORCED
OFF TABLE</td>
<td>(b)</td>
<td>Any ball which is forced off the table becomes out of play, but, with the exception of a red ball, is immediately replaced upon its allotted spot.</td>
</tr>
<tr>
<td>BALL 'ON'.
TO PLAY
AT BALLS</td>
<td>(c)</td>
<td>A player is said to be *on* a ball when such ball may be lawfully struck by the cue ball under these Rules. He is *on* a pool ball nominated under Rules 5 and 10.</td>
</tr>
<tr>
<td>PLAYER
SNOOKERED</td>
<td>(d)</td>
<td>A player is said to be *snookered* with regard to any ball when a direct stroke in a straight line of the cue ball to any point of such ball is obstructed by any ball which is not *on.* If a player is *in hand* after a foul, he cannot be *snookered* with regard to any ball that is *on,* if he can get a direct stroke in a straight line from some part of the 'D' (*i.e.,* a clear ball).</td>
</tr>
</table>

When the ball *on* is snookered by more than one ball, the effective snookering ball is the one nearest to the cue ball.

(e) The cue ball is said to be *angled* when the corner of the cushion prevents a stroke being made, in a straight line, directly on any part of all balls that may be lawfully struck.

(f) A *Nominated Ball* is the object ball which the striker declares he undertakes to strike with the first impact of the cue ball.

4. Fifteen reds in the form of a triangle, the ball at the apex standing as near to the pink ball as possible, without touching it; the base being parallel with and nearest to the top cushion: BLACK on the BILLIARD SPOT; PINK on the PYRAMID SPOT; BLUE on the CENTRE SPOT; BROWN on the MIDDLE of the Baulk-line; GREEN on the LEFT-HAND and YELLOW on the RIGHT-HAND corner of the 'D'.

5. Players must first determine by lot, or other convenient method, the order of their turn, which must remain unaltered throughout the game. The first player shall play from hand. The cue ball shall strike a red as the initial stroke of each turn, until all the reds are off the table. The value of each red, lawfully pocketed by the same stroke, is scored. For the next stroke of the turn (if a score is made) the cue ball shall strike a pool ball, the value of which (if lawfully pocketed) is scored. The game is continued by pocketing reds, and pool balls, alternately, in the same turn. If the striker fails to score, the player next in turn plays from where the cue ball came to rest. If the cue ball

is pocketed or forced off the table, the next player plays from hand. Once the cue ball has come to rest on the table after a foul has been committed it must be played from where it has come to rest. Each *pool ball* pocketed or forced off

the table, must be re-spotted before the next stroke, until finally pocketed under these Rules. If the player who lawfully pockets the last red, pocket any pool ball with his next

stroke, this ball is re-spotted. Otherwise (reds being off the table) the pool balls must be struck by the cue ball in the progressive order of their values, and *if lawfully pocketed* are not re-spotted. When requested by the referee a player must state which ball he is *on*. He is advised to do so for his own protection. An intentional miss shall not be made. The player shall, to the best of his ability, endeavour to strike a ball that is *on*.

The first impact of the cue ball shall govern all strokes.

EXAMPLE. A player *on* blue makes the first impact with the cue ball on the blue, the cue ball then strikes the black or any other ball and goes into a pocket, the player is penalised five points, the value of the blue, the ball on which the cue ball made the first impact.

6. The scoring values of the balls are: red=1, yellow=2, green=3, brown=4, blue=5, pink=6, black=7.

7. The striker must see that every ball required to be re-spotted is properly placed before he plays his stroke. *Reds* are never re-spotted. Any pool ball pocketed by a foul stroke is not deemed to have been lawfully pocketed, and shall be re-spotted. If the spot, named in Rule 4 for each pool ball, is occupied when such ball shall be placed thereon, the ball shall be placed on the spot first named in Rule 4, that is then unoccupied, *i.e.*, if the spot allocated to the yellow is occupied by another ball, after the yellow has been pocketed, then the yellow ball is to be placed on the black spot, or, if that is occupied, then on the pink spot, and so on. If all the spots are occupied, any pool ball other than the black and pink shall be placed as near its own spot as possible between that spot and the *nearest part* of the top cushion without touching another ball. In the case of the black and pink balls being potted and all the spots are occupied, they shall be placed as near as possible to their own spots, up the table, on the centre line of the table, and without touching another ball. If the space between the black spot and the top cushion is occupied, the black ball shall be placed as near as possible to the black spot, on the centre line of the table, below its spot, and without touching another ball. Similarly if the space between the pink spot and the top cushion is occupied, the pink shall be placed as near as possible to the pink spot, on the centre line of the table, below its spot, and without touching another ball.

BALLS STRUCK	8.	Two balls (other than two reds or the ball *on* and the ball nominated under Rule 10) must not be struck simultaneously nor pocketed by the same stroke.
SIMULTANEOUSLY OR		
POCKETED IN ONE		
STROKE		

8. Two balls (other than two reds or the ball *on* and the ball nominated under Rule 10) must not be struck simultaneously nor pocketed by the same stroke.

NOTE: Any number of red balls may be pocketed by one stroke made in accordance with these rules.

CUE BALL
TOUCHING

9. (a) If the cue ball is touching another ball which is *on,* the striker must play away from the touching ball without moving the latter, or he must be held to have pushed. The striker thus playing away from a ball *on* shall incur no penalty for a miss or for striking another ball, but he may lawfully pocket any other ball which is *on*. If he pockets a ball which is not *on*, he forfeits the penalty under Rule 12.

(b) If the cue ball is touching another ball which is not *on*, the striker must play away from such ball as in (a). If the ball *on* is missed, or another ball hit, the penalty as laid down in Rule 12 must be forfeited.

(c) In all cases where the cue ball is touching the ball *on* or touching a colour after a red has been potted, the referee shall state 'TOUCHING BALL' without being asked. If the cue ball is touching more than one ball *on* he shall, on request, state which ball(s) the cue ball is touching. He shall offer no other information.

EXAMPLES: (1) The *ball on is red,* cue ball is *touching red,* striker plays away from red without disturbing it, strikes and goes in off black. The penalty is four points, the value of the ball *on*.

(2) The *ball on is yellow,* cue ball is *touching yellow,* striker plays away from yellow without disturbing it, and pockets black. The penalty is seven points, the value of the ball *pocketed*.

(3) The *ball on is red,* cue ball is *touching black,* striker plays away from black without disturbing it, misses all balls and cue ball enters a pocket. The penalty is four points, the value of the ball *on*.

(4) In the case of the striker, playing away from black, missing all reds and striking blue he is penalised five points.

SNOOKERING AFTER
A FOUL

10. After a foul stroke, if the striker be snookered, (a) *with regard to all reds*, he is then *on* any ball he may nominate, and for all purposes such nominated ball shall be regarded as a red, except that, if pocketed, it shall be spotted.

(b) After a foul stroke, if the striker be snookered (*reds being off the table*), *with regard to the pool ball on,* he is then *on* any ball he may nominate, and for all purposes such nominated ball shall be regarded as the ball *on,* except that should it be lawfully pocketed it shall be spotted, and the player shall continue his break on the ball he was *on,* but for being snookered. If, as a result of playing on the nominated ball, the ball *on* be pocketed, it shall be scored and the player continues his break. Should both the nominated ball and the ball *on* be pocketed by the same stroke, only the ball *on* shall be scored, and the player continues his break. The nominated ball only shall be re-spotted.

Should the striker leave the opponent snookered by the nominated ball it is a foul stroke, except when only pink and black remain on the table.

Should the striker fail to hit the ball nominated under this Rule it is a foul stroke.

11. If the cue ball is angled it must be played from where it lies; but if angled after a foul, it may be played from hand, at the striker's discretion.

12. A player who contravenes any Rule of this game *(a)* cannot score; *(b)* loses his turn; *(c)* forfeits such points as are exacted in these Rules – which are added to his opponent's score; *(d)* in addition, the striker has the option of playing from where the balls have come to rest, or requesting the opponent to play the stroke; *(e)* minimum penalty for any infringement is four points.

13. The player contravenes these rules by the following acts (among others): –
    (a) By making a losing hazard. Penalty, value of ball *on,* or value of ball struck, whichever is the higher.
    (b) By causing the cue ball to strike a ball he is not *on.* Penalty, value of the ball struck, or value of the ball *on,* whichever is the higher.
    (c) By making a miss. Penalty, value of ball *on.*
    (d) By snookering his opponent with the nominated ball after a foul stroke, except when only pink and black remain. Penalty, value of the ball *on.*
    (e) By striking simultaneously or pocketing with one stroke two balls, except two reds, or the ball *on* and the ball nominated. Penalty, highest value of the two struck, or pocketed.

(f) By moving an object ball in contravention of Rule 9 (Cue ball Touching). Penalty, value of the ball *on*, or value of the ball moved, whichever is the higher.

(g) By forcing a ball off the table. Penalty, the value of the ball *on* or the value of the ball forced off the table, whichever is the higher.

(h) By pocketing any ball not *on*. Penalty, value of the ball pocketed, or value of the ball *on*, whichever is the higher.

(i) For playing with other than the cue ball. Penalty, seven points.

(j) By playing at two reds in successive strokes. Penalty, seven points.

(k) By using a dead ball to test whether a ball will pass another, or go on a spot, or for any other purpose. Penalty, seven points.

(l) By playing with both feet off the floor. Penalty – value of the ball *on*, or value of the ball struck, or value of the ball pocketed or value of the ball improperly spotted, whichever is the higher.

(m) By playing before the balls have come to rest, or before they have been spotted or when wrongly spotted. Penalty, value of the ball *on*, or value of the ball struck, or value of the ball wrongly spotted, or value of the ball pocketed, whichever is the higher.

(n) By striking or touching a ball whilst in play, otherwise than with the tip of the cue. Penalty, value of the *ball struck* or *touched,* or value of the ball *on*, whichever is the higher.

(o) By playing improperly from hand. Penalty, value of the ball *on*, or value of the ball struck, or value of the ball pocketed, or value of the ball improperly spotted, whichever is the higher.

(p) Push Stroke. Penalty, value of the ball *on*, or value of the ball struck, or value of the ball pocketed, whichever is the higher.

(q) Jump Shot. Penalty, value of the ball *on*, or value of the ball struck, or value of the ball pocketed, whichever is the higher.

(r) By playing out of turn. Penalty, value of the ball *on*, or value of the ball struck, or value of the ball pocketed, whichever is the higher.

Only the referee is allowed to clean a ball on the table. He should do so at a player's request.

It is the striker's responsibility to see that the balls are correctly spotted before playing his stroke.

If the referee considers that a player is taking an abnormal amount of time over his stroke, with the intention of upsetting his opponent, the referee should warn him that he runs the risk of being disqualified if he pursues these tactics.

A player should not be penalised if, when using the rest, the rest head falls off and touches a ball.

Unless a foul stroke is awarded by the referee, or claimed by the non-striker, before the next stroke is made, it is condoned.

If the striker plays with the balls improperly spotted, he scores all points made until the foul is awarded by the referee, or claimed by the non-striker.

The referee should not give any indication that a player is about to make a foul stroke.

If the striker makes a miss, the referee can order him to replay the stroke penalising him the requisite forfeit for each miss, but he scores all points in any subsequent stroke.

When awarded a free ball a player need only nominate the ball he intends to play, when requested to do so by the referee.

If at the opening stroke of a game the striker fails to hit a red, the next player plays from where the cue ball has come to rest .

A SNOOKER

A player must be able to strike both sides of the ball *on* free of obstruction from any ball or balls not *on*. It virtually means the diameter of a ball on either side of the ball *on*.

If a player is colour blind, the referee should tell him the colour of a ball if requested.

A referee must declare when a player has a free ball without appeal from a player.

EXAMPLES OF FOUL STROKES

EXAMPLES: (1) *Red is the ball on,* striker fouls *the black* with his cue or otherwise, the penalty is seven points, the value of the *ball fouled.*

(2) *Black is the ball on,* striker fouls *a red* with his cue or arm, the penalty is seven points, the value of the *ball on.*

(3) A player pots the *pink* and before it is properly spotted he pots a *red* ball – what is the penalty?

Decision: 6 points for playing with the balls not properly spotted (value of the ball not properly spotted).

<table>
<tr><td>WILFUL EVASION OF
SPIRIT OF RULES</td><td></td><td>If a game is awarded to a player under Rule 15 GENERAL RULES, the offender shall lose the game, and forfeit all points he may have scored, or the value of the balls on the table (red = 8 each) whichever is higher.</td></tr>
<tr><td>END OF GAME
AND TIE</td><td>14.</td><td>When only the black ball is left, the first score or forfeit ends the game, unless the scores are then equal, in which case the black is spotted, and the players draw lots for choice of playing at the black from hand. The next score or forfeit ends the game. In games (whether individuals, pairs or teams) where aggregate points decide the winner, it is only when the scores are equal as a result of the last frame, that the black is re-spotted. The next score or forfeit ends the game.</td></tr>
<tr><td>FOUR-HANDED
SNOOKER</td><td></td><td>Rules of Snooker apply.</td></tr>
</table>

In a four-handed match at snooker whether it be on frames or on aggregate points, each side shall open alternative frames, but the order of play shall be determined at the commencement of each frame. Players may change order of play at the beginning of each frame which must be maintained throughout that frame.

If a foul is committed and a request is made to play again, the player who committed the foul plays again, and the order of play is maintained.

When a game ends in a tie Snooker Rule 14 is applied. The pair who play the first stroke have the choice as to which player plays that stroke. The order of play must be maintained as in the frame.

General Rules

These General Rules, Technical Terms and Laws apply to Games played on an English Billiard Table

Authorised by The Billiards and Snooker Control Council

The Table

<table>
<tr><td>MEASUREMENTS</td><td>1.</td><td>The B. & S.C.C. 12 ft. Standard Table: The slate bed of the table shall measure 12 ft. by 6 ft. 1½ in. The edge of the cushions shall not project over the slate more than</td></tr>
<tr><td>HEIGHT</td><td></td><td>2 in. or less than 1½ in. The height of the table, from the floor to the top of the cushion rail, shall be from 2 ft. 9½ in. to 2 ft. 10½ in. There shall be pockets at the corners</td></tr>
</table>

(the two at the Baulk end being known as the bottom pockets and the two at the spot end as the top pockets) and at the middle of the longer sides, and the pocket opening shall conform to the templates authorised by The Billiards and Snooker Control Council.

A straight line drawn 29 inches from the face of the bottom cushion and parallel to it is called the Baulk-line, and the intervening space is termed the Baulk. The 'D' is a semi-circle described in baulk, with its centre at the middle of the baulk-line, and with a radius of 11½ inches.

Spots MARKED on the table are:

(a) THE SPOT, 12¾ inches from a point perpendicular below the face of the top cushion on the centre longitudinal line of the table;

(b) THE CENTRE SPOT, mid-way between the middle pockets;

(c) THE PYRAMID SPOT, mid-way between the CENTRE SPOT and the face of the top cushion; and

(d) THE MIDDLE OF THE BAULK-LINE—all four being on the centre longitudinal line of the table.

I. (a) The B. & S.C.C. 6 ft. Standard Table.—The slate bed of the table shall be not less than ½ in. in thickness and shall measure 6 ft. by 3 ft. 1½ in. The edge of the cushions shall project over the slate 1½ in. There shall be pockets at the corners and at the middle of the long sides, and the pocket openings shall conform to the templates authorised by The Billiards and Snooker Control Council for 6 ft. standard tables.

A straight line drawn 14½ inches from the face of the bottom cushion and parallel to it is called the Baulk-line, and the intervening space is termed the Baulk. The 'D' is a semi-circle described in Baulk, with its centre at the middle of the Baulk-line and with a radius of 5¾ inches.

Spots MARKED on the table are:

(a) THE SPOT, 7 inches from a point perpendicular below the face of the top cushion on the centre longitudinal line of the table;

(b) THE CENTRE SPOT, mid-way between the middle pockets;

(c) THE PYRAMID SPOT, mid-way between the CENTRE SPOT and the face of the top cushion; and

(d) THE MIDDLE OF THE BAULK-LINE—all four being on the centre longitudinal line of the table.

Balls

MEASUREMENTS

2. The B. & S.C.C. 12 ft. Standard Table balls should be of equal size and weight, and of a diameter of $2\frac{1}{16}$ inches, within manufacturers' tolerance.

The B. & S.C.C. 6 ft. Standard Table balls should be of equal size and weight, and of a diameter of $1\frac{7}{8}$ inches, within manufacturers' tolerance.

The Cue

2. (a) A Billiard Cue as recognised by the B. & S. C.C. shall be not less than three feet in length and shall show no substantial departure from the traditional and generally accepted shape and form.

Technical Terms

TO STRING

3. (a) To string is to play together from the Baulk-line to the top cushion with the object of leaving player's ball as near as possible to the bottom cushion.

CUE BALL

(b) The cue ball is the ball of the striker; all other balls are object balls.

BALL IN HAND

(c) A player's ball is *in hand* when it is off the table.

TO PLAY FROM HAND

(d) To play from hand the striker must play the cue ball from some position on or within the lines of the 'D'.

BALL IN BAULK

(e) A ball is *in baulk* when it rests on the Baulk-line or between that line and the bottom cushion.

BALL OFF THE TABLE

(f) A ball is *forced off the table* which comes to rest otherwise than on the bed of the table or in a pocket.

STRIKER AND
NON-STRIKER

(g) The person about to play or in play is termed the *Striker;* his opponent is the *Non-Striker.*

BALL IN PLAY

(h) The ball of the striker is *in play* when it has been finally place on the table and struck with the tip of the cue (or spotted under the Rules of the game being played), and remains so until pocketed. The ball of the non-striker is *in play* when it has been spotted under the Rules of the game being played. Other balls are in play when spotted and remain so until pocketed.

Any ball which is forced off the table becomes out of play.

A STROKE	(i)	A Stroke is made by a player touching his ball, or striking his ball when it is in play, with the tip of his cue. No stroke is completed until all the balls have come to rest and the player is adjudged to have left the table.
A BREAK	(j)	A Break is a series of consecutive scoring strokes made in any one turn.
A CANNON	(k)	A Cannon is made when the striker's ball makes contact with two other balls.
WINNING HAZARD	(l)	A Winning Hazard is made when a ball, other than the cue ball is pocketed after contact with another ball
LOSING HAZARD	(m)	A Losing Hazard is made when the cue ball is pocketed after contact with another ball.
A MISS	(n)	A Miss is a stroke where the cue ball fails to touch any other ball; or in Billiards where the cue ball, when played from hand, strikes any part of a ball in baulk without first hitting a ball or cushion out of baulk; or where the cue ball is struck more than once before contact with another ball.
SPOT OCCUPIED	(o)	A spot or position is said to be *occupied* if a ball cannot be placed thereon without touching or disturbing another ball.
THE FALL	(p)	The curved edge of the bed of the table forming the mouth of the pocket is called the fall.
FIRST IMPACT OF CUE BALL	4.	The first impact of the cue ball shall govern all strokes.
BALL PROPERLY SPOTTED	5.	A ball is not considered to be spotted unless it has been placed by hand on its prescribed spot.
A FAIR STROKE	6.	All strokes must be made with the tip of the cue. The ball must be struck, and not pushed. The ball must not be struck more than once in the same stroke either before or after contact with another ball. At the moment of striking, one of the player's feet must touch the floor. A ball or balls must not be forced off the table.
A FOUL STROKE	7.	A foul stroke is one made in contravention of any Rule of the game being played (see Sectional Rules).

187

BALL ON EDGE OF POCKET	8.	If the ball which falls is part of the stroke, that stroke shall be void, the balls placed in their original position and the stroke replayed. If the ball is not an integral part of the stroke, the stroke shall stand and the ball which fell only shall be replaced. If it balances momentarily on the edge and fall in, it must not be replaced.
BALL MOVED BY OTHER AGENCY THAN PLAYER	9.	If a ball is disturbed otherwise than by the player, it shall, if moved, be placed on the table by the referee on the spot which, in his judgment, the ball had, or if moving, would have occupied. This rule covers the case in which a non-striker or non-player causes the striker to touch or move a ball. The player shall not be responsible for any disturbance of the balls by the referee or by the marker.
CONDUCT OF NON-STRIKER	· 10.	The non-striker shall, when the striker is playing, avoid standing or moving in the line of sight; he should sit or stand at a fair distance from the table. He may, in case of his enforced absence from the room, appoint a substitute to watch his interests, and claim a foul if necessary.
PENALTIES	11.	If during a stroke any rule is contravened the striker (a) cannot score, (b) loses his turn, (c) forfeits such points as are exacted under the Rules of the game being played.
BALLS CHANGED	12.	The set of balls may be changed during a game, by consent of the players or by decision of the referee.
ORDER OF TURN COMMENCEMENT OF GAME	13.	The players shall determine the order of play by stringing or by lot; the order of play shall remain unaltered throughout the game. The game does not commence until the cue ball has been finally placed on the table and struck with the tip of the cue, by the first player.
THE REFEREE	14.	(a) The Referee shall be the sole judge of fair or unfair play, and shall be responsible for the proper conduct of the game under these Rules, and shall, of his own initiative, intervene if he sees any contravention. He shall, on appeal by a player, and on appeal only, decide any question of fact connected with play. (The referee on appeal if a ball is in or out of baulk shall only give a decision when the player is in hand.)

(EXAMPLES: If a ball touch the striker's ball; if it is properly placed to play from hand; or if properly spotted.)

If he has failed to observe any incident, he may take the evidence of the spectators best placed for observation, to assist his decision.

He shall decide all questions arising between the players on the interpretations of these rules.

The referee shall not give any advice or express opinion on points affecting play.

(EXAMPLES: The referee should not offer an opinion as to whether there is room for a ball to be spotted if pocketed by a stroke about to be played. If the striker plays from hand outside the limits of the 'D', the referee shall not warn him before the stroke is played, but shall award the foul immediately afterwards.)

THE MARKER   14. (b) The Marker shall keep the score on the marking board, and assist the referee to carry out his duties.

PLAYER'S CONDUCT   15. For refusing to continue the game when called upon by the referee to do so, or for conduct which, in the opinion of the referee, is wilfully or persistently unfair, a player shall lose the game, and is liable to be disqualified for any future competition held under the control of The Billiards Association and Control Council, or its Affiliated Associations.

THE SPECTATORS   16. Spectators should not interfere with the game, the players, the marker, or the referee.

THE PUSH STROKE   A Push Stroke is a foul and is made when (A) the tip of the cue remains in contact with the cue ball when the cue ball makes contact with the object ball, or when (B) the tip of the cue remains in contact with the cue ball after the cue ball has commenced its forward motion. Penalty in Billiards: None. In conjunction with a miss one away. In Snooker: Value of the ball 'on', or value of the ball struck, or value of the ball pocketed, whichever is the higher.

THE JUMP SHOT   The Jump Shot is a foul in which the cue ball is made to jump over any ball whether by accident or design. Penalty in Billiards: None. In conjunction with a miss, one away. In Snooker: Value of the ball 'on', or value of the ball struck, or value of the ball pocketed, whichever is the higher.

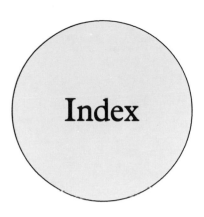

Index

For a list of Lessons *See* Contents Part I — page 15
For a List of Trick Shots *See* Contents Part II — page 103